AF348632

NAYLA ROMANOS ILIYA

THE PHOENICIAN ALPHABET

EDITED BY ROSE ISSA
TEXTS BY PROF. SUSSAN BABAIE
AND SIR PETER MURRAY

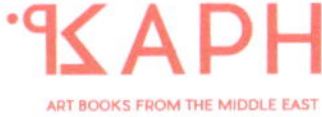

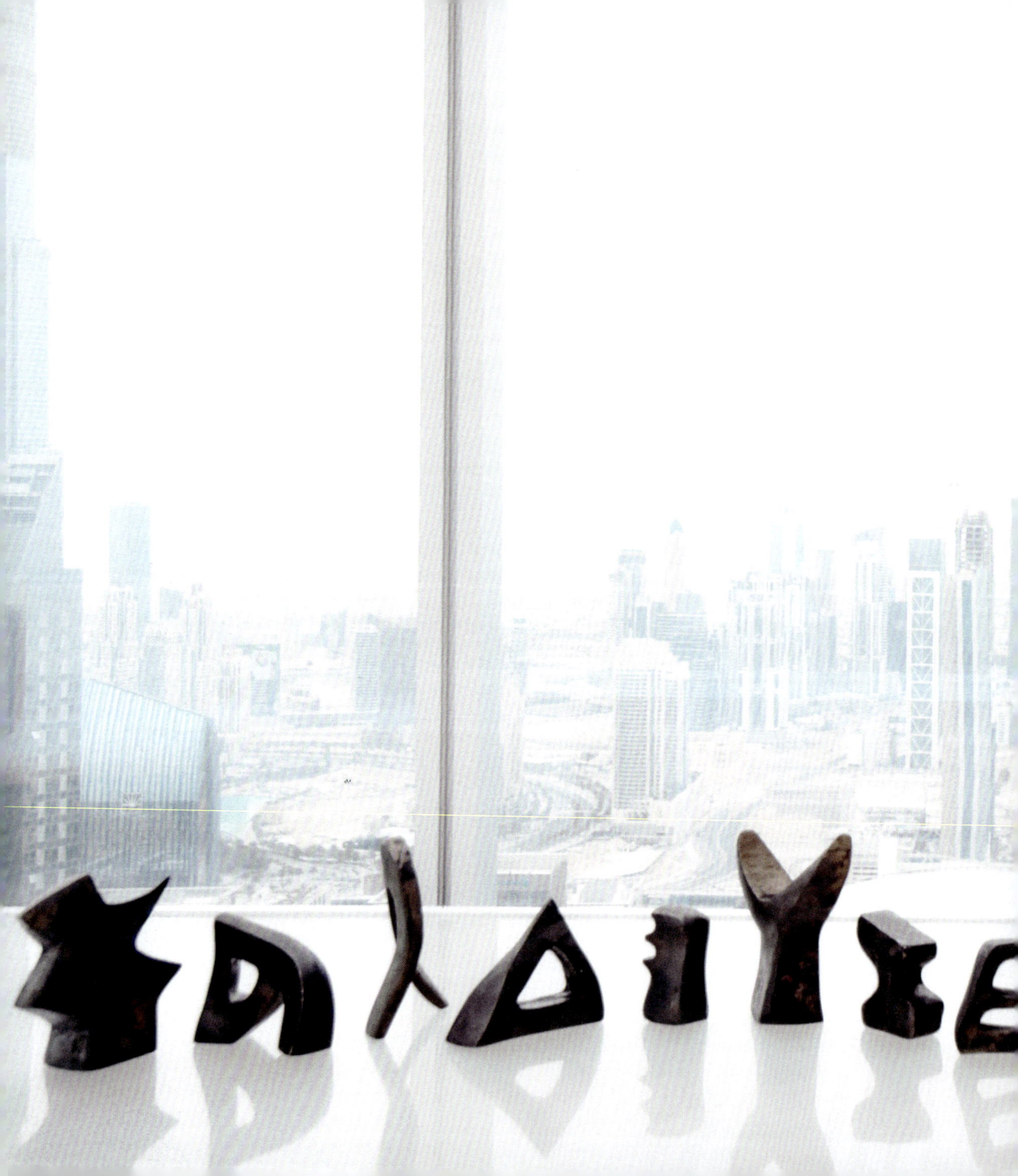

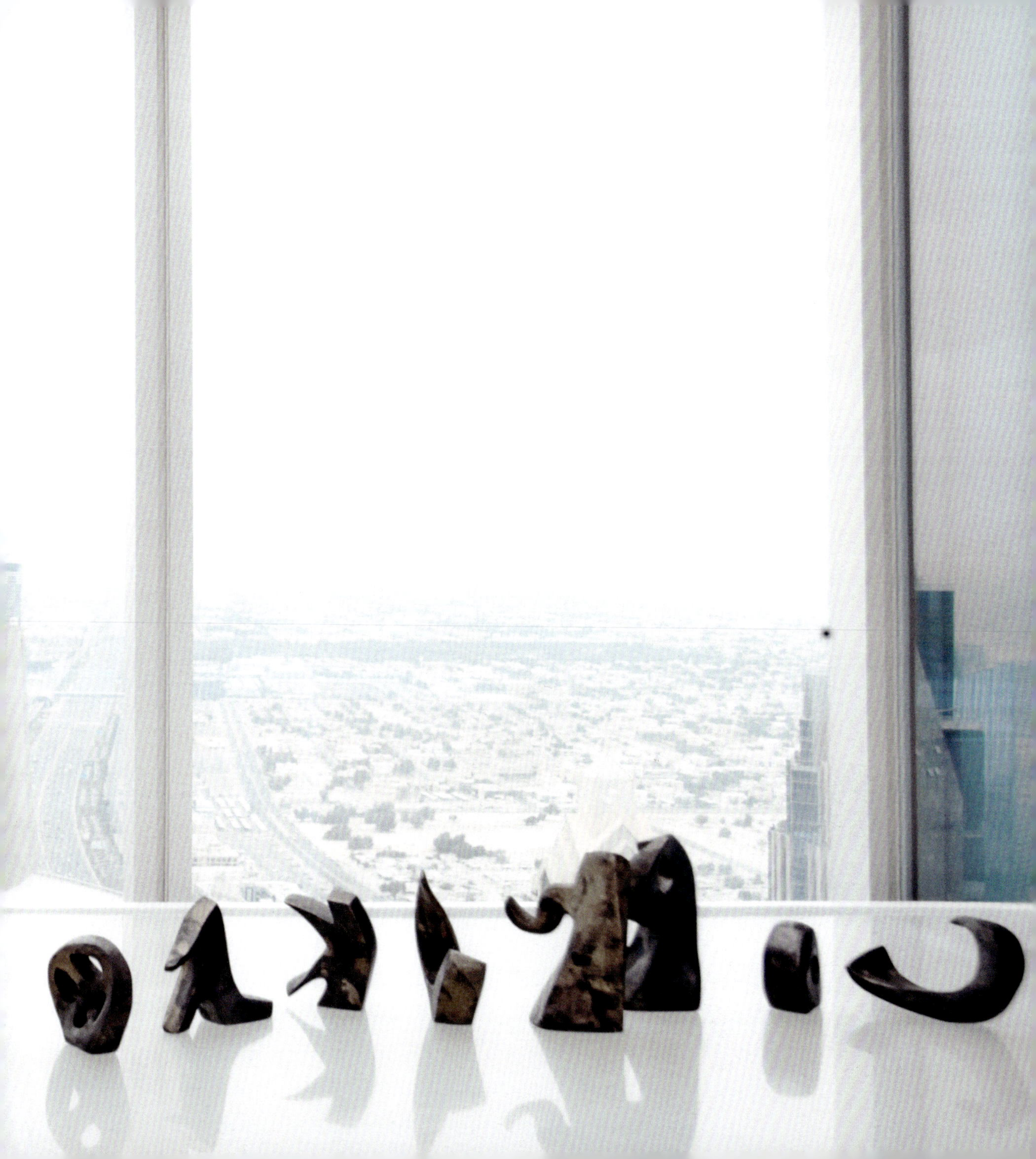

CONTENTS

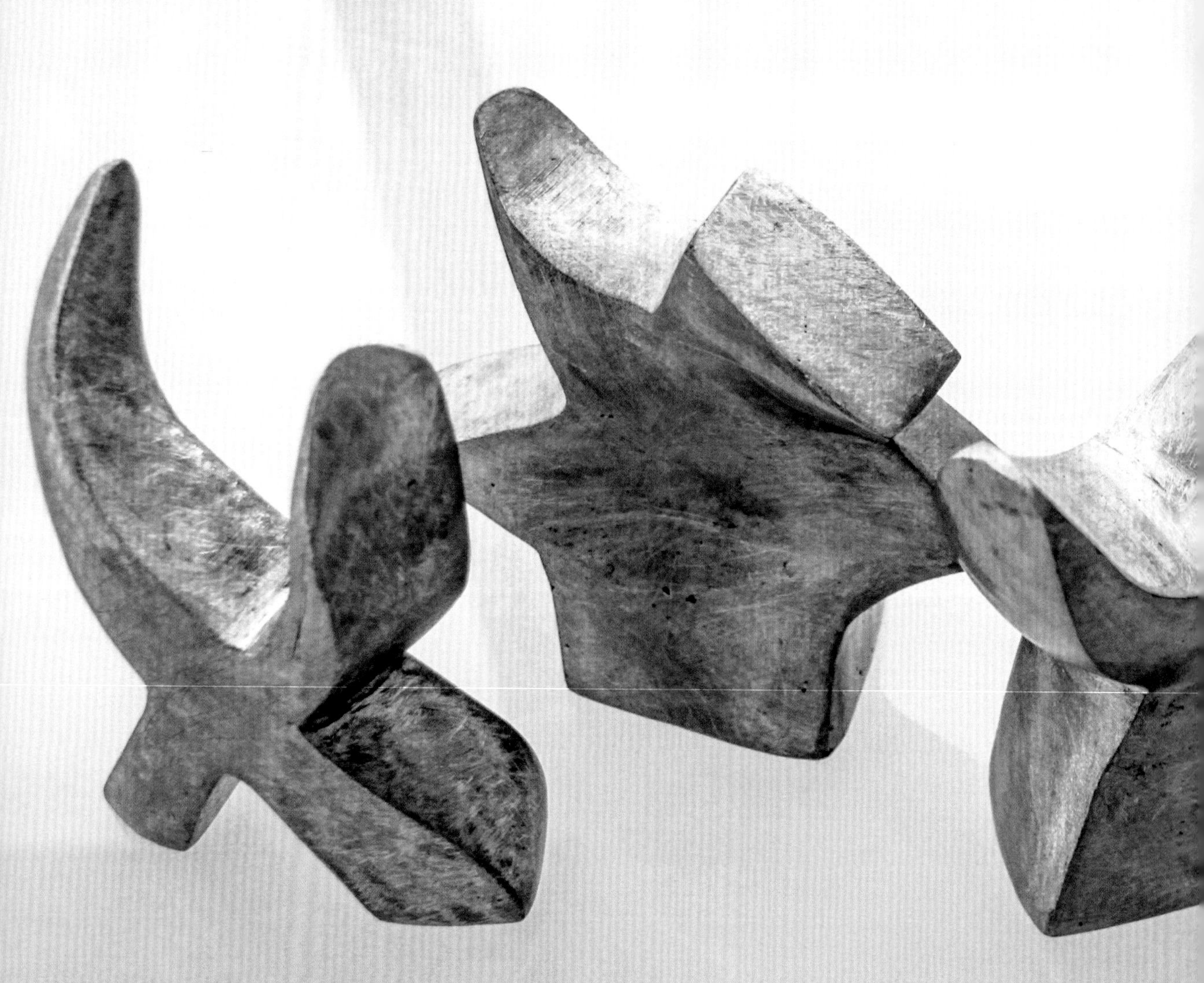

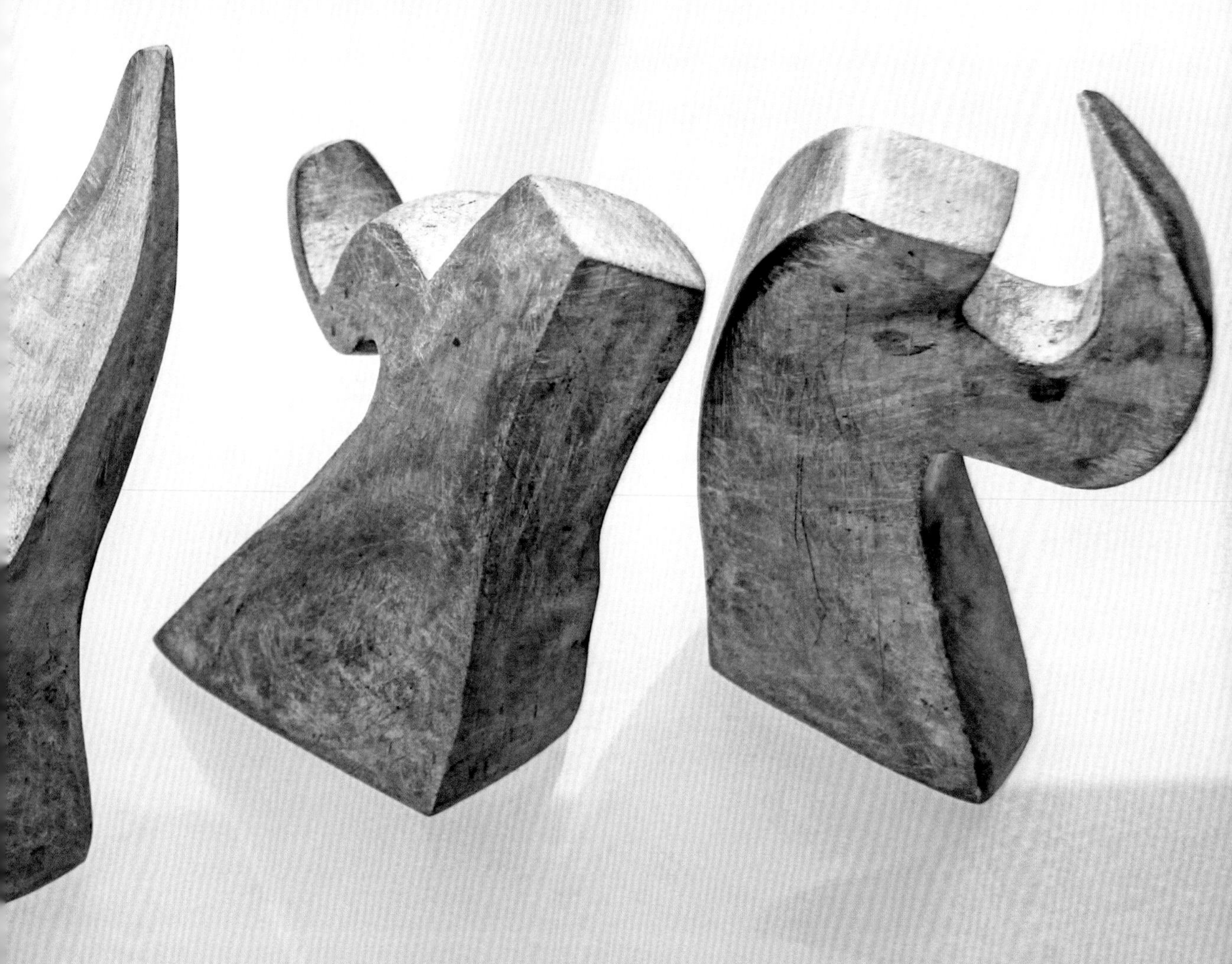

'ARCHITECTURE AND ART SHARE

A BLURRY FRONTIER, AND THIS IS

WHERE I COME FROM. I GOT INTO

SCULPTURE VIA ARCHITECTURE, AND

APPROACH IT AS SUCH, REPLACING

FUNCTION WITH INTUITION. I AM OFTEN

ASKED IF IT IS MORE GRATIFYING TO

BE AN ARCHITECT OR A SCULPTOR—

I THINK BOTH PRACTICES PROVIDE

ME WITH THE SAME SENSE OF
SATISFACTION IN THE END, BUT I VERY
MUCH PREFER BEING A SCULPTOR.
I FEEL BLESSED TO BE ABLE TO USE,
CONVEY, AND WORK OFF MY FEELINGS
THROUGH ART. THE PROCESS IS
OFTEN THERAPEUTIC, ALWAYS
LIBERATING: ME ALONE, CREATING
SOMETHING, FREE.'

Language is not unique to humans, but human language is unique. The human ability to use language in an infinite variety of creative ways to spin and tell stories is distinctive.

Nayla Romanos Iliya shares her story as an artist via childhood sound experiences and linguistic exposures. Her life journey is both familiar and unique, a Lebanese at home in exploring the sounds and shapes of an ancient language to which she has anchored the fluid idea of selfhood. An architect by training, she possesses an inclination toward spatial articulation of forms that is profoundly influential in her work. She makes sculptures of shapes that convey resonances of the Phoenician alphabet, an extinct language whose earliest known inscriptions come from Byblos, Lebanon.

The Phoenician people were great navigators, and their instinct for trade brought them into contact with a vast region of the ancient world, from the Levant to the Mediterranean coast, from Tyre to Carthage. Through commerce and colonisation, the Phoenician script spread, and its alphabet formed the basis of most languages still alive today, including Arabic and Latin derived languages. This script with only twenty-two consonants and no marks for vowels has become the story told by Nayla Romanos Iliya in her Phoenician alphabet series. The works reimagine the ancient language in three-dimensional, space-occupying volumes of sounds. Each piece invites the viewer to see the mass of the letters while also asking us to produce the tonality out of the negative space within which the sculptures exist. Calligraphic arts have inspired many contemporary artists, some of whom have powerfully deployed the volumetric and the monumental shapes of letters and words, like the artist Parviz Tanavoli in his famous *Heech* (*Nothingness*) series. Nayla Romanos Iliya's letters, in their graphical shapes, act as visually imagined representations of sounds. As such, her work offers one of the most fascinating interventions of the creative mind into one of the greatest inventions of human beings.

PROF. SUSSAN BABAIE
The Courtauld Institute of Art, University of London

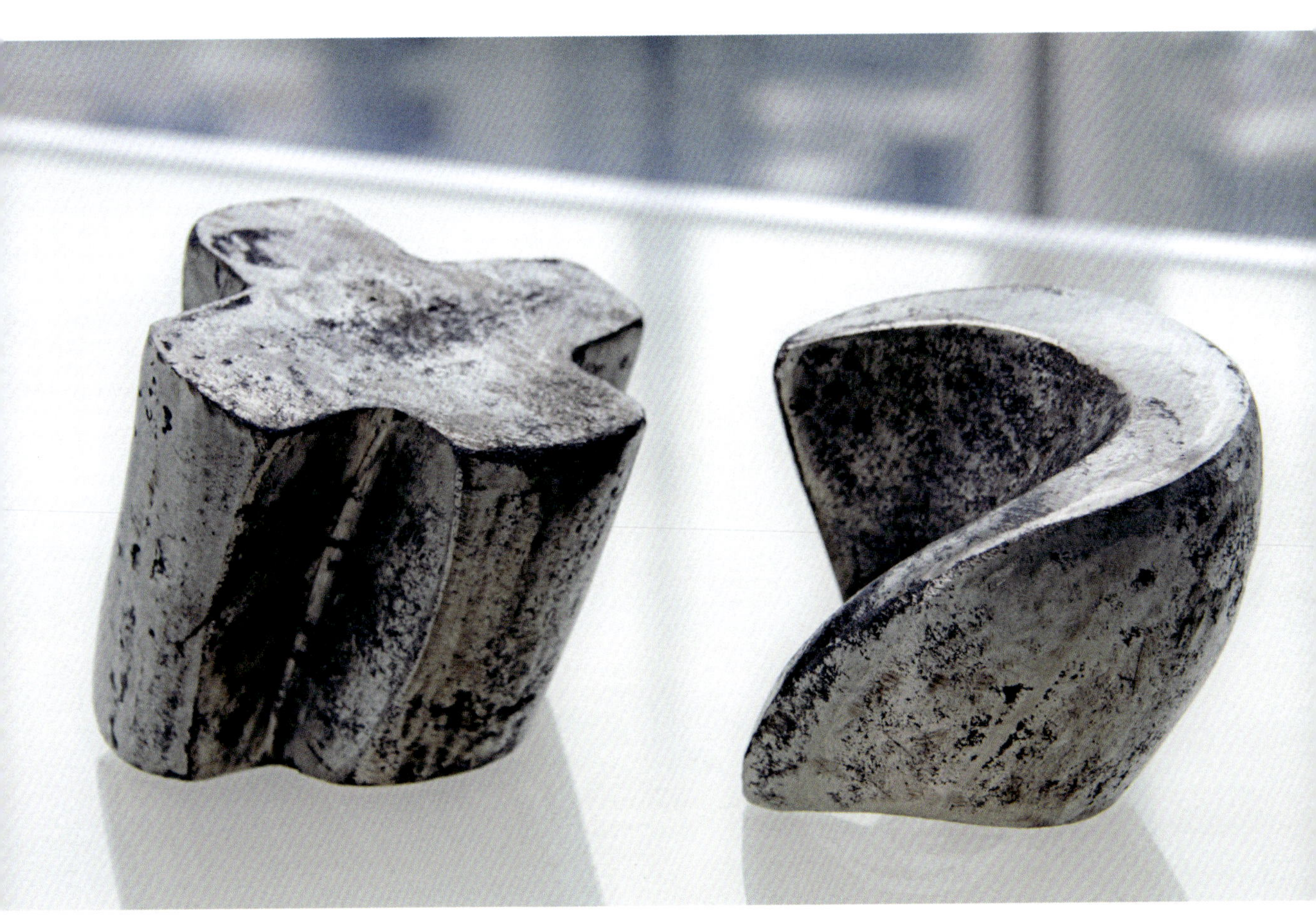

TETH AND **L3D**, 2013

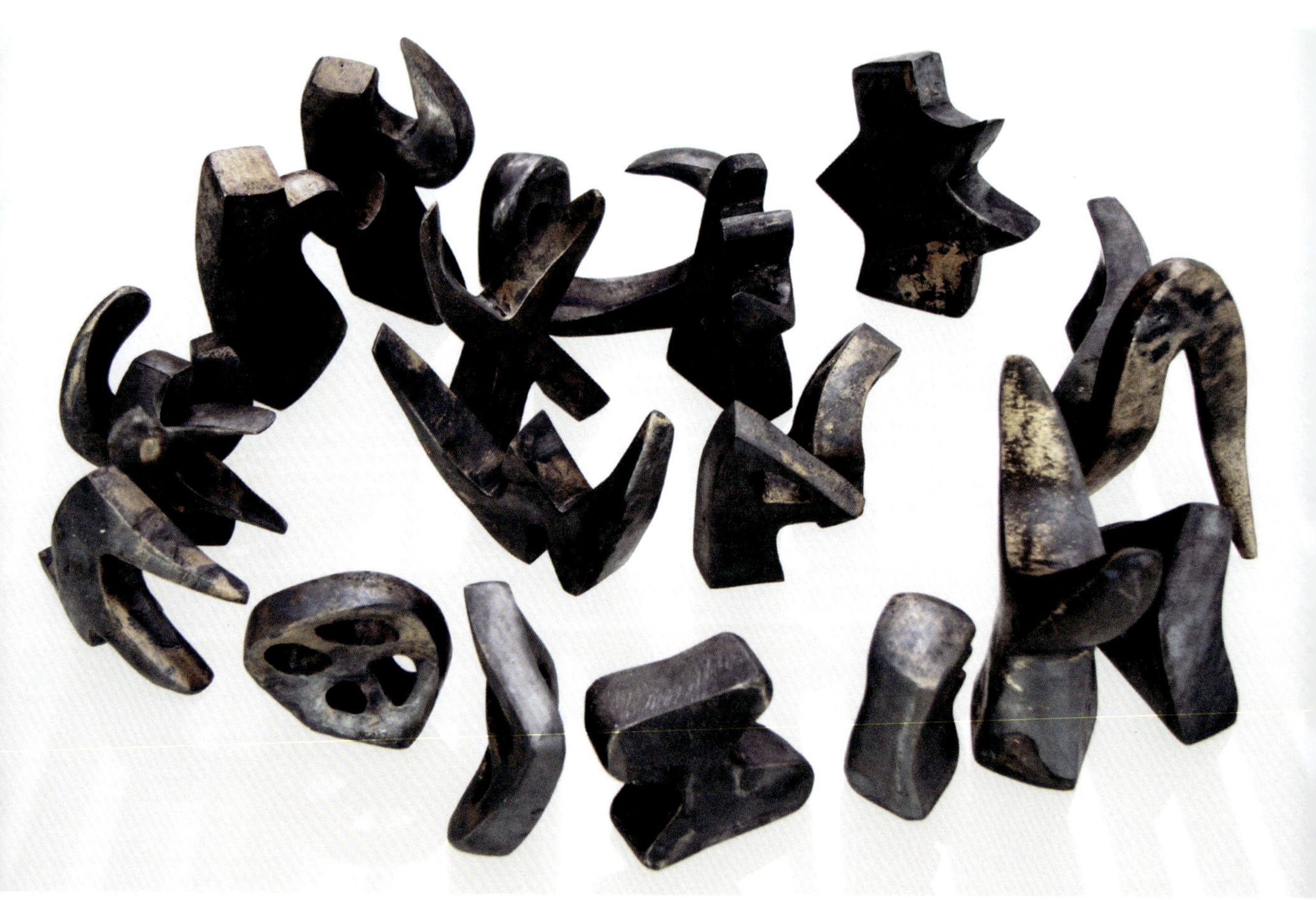

1ST PROTOTYPES, 2012

Born in Geneva in 1857, Ferdinand de Saussure spent much of his life studying Sanskrit and reconstructing the sounds of Proto-Indo-European language systems. De Saussure chose Sanskrit not least because it was believed to be the oldest human language in existence: one from which many, if not all, other languages were descended. In 1878, aged just 21, he published *Mémoire sur le système primitif des voyelles dans les langues indo-européennes* (*Essay on the Original System of Vowels in the Indo-European Languages*). However, his best-known work, *Course in Linguistics*, was compiled and published after his death in 1916. De Saussure held that human language can be analysed as a structured system of 'signs', which in turn can be separated into two elements: signifiers, where the sound creates an immediate image, and that which is signified—i.e. the concept or meaning intended. Saussure preferred a synchronic approach, one which looked at the structure of language as it exists today, without delving into history. The signs themselves, he held, although once significant, had become arbitrary over the passage of years, their original meaning dissipated.

In more traditional approaches to researching the origin of language, it was believed that the further one looked back, the closer was the connection between the naming of a thing and the thing named. Old language possesses an elemental power, and the Phoenician alphabet, in use over 3,000 years ago, is one of the oldest. The bronze sculptures of Nayla Romanos Iliya, based on the letters of the Phoenician alphabet, set out to rediscover this power, and to reinvest meaning into signs nearly as old as human civilisation itself. The twenty-two letters of the Phoenician alphabet, beginning Aleph, Beth, Ghimel and Daleth, are a window into the world of the Old Testament. Romanos Iliya's work invites contemporary viewers to put aside for a moment the struggle to understand differences in these tightly contested geographical areas, and to remember the ebb and flow of history, the migrations of peoples and settlements, and the displacements, often accompanied by conflict, that have taken place over many thousands of years in this cradle of human civilisation.

De Saussure, in his *Course in Linguistics*, observed that Phoenician, used in ancient times in Lebanon and Syria, had survived into Roman times. In a comedy by Plautus, *Poenulus* or *The Young Carthaginians*, written around 190 BC, Hanno from Carthage speaks lines in Phoenician, which Plautus then translates. But, when Plautus was writing, Phoenician was an archaic language, its alphabet having given way to Greek, which in turn gave way to Latin. However, most of the letters of the Roman alphabet used today owe their form, and what is left of their symbolic meaning, to the Phoenicians. Two thousand years before Plautus wrote his play, the Phoenicians were adventuring seafarers, who established colonies along the coast of North Africa—in Tunisia, Morocco and Libya—as well as on the Mediterranean islands of Malta, Sicily and Sardinia. Many eighteenth-century antiquarians, such as Charles Vallancey and William Jones, believed that these seafarers, sailing from their capital city of Tyre, or from their colony at Carthage, had been among the original settlers of Britain and Ireland. While this theory is no longer adhered to, neither has it ever been disproved.

Although no Phoenician papyri have survived, the main sources for knowledge of the language comes from inscriptions, coins and pottery fragments. In 1694 two boundary stones were discovered in Malta. Referred to as the Cippi of Melqart, the stones bear bilingual inscriptions; thus, by the same method that applied in the case of the Rosetta Stone, they enabled French linguist Jean-Jacques Barthélemy to decipher the Phoenician language and alphabet. He discovered that the script is written right to left, the symbols representing syllables rather than pictures. A Semitic language, Phoenician is related to Hebrew and works on the principle that the letters of the alphabet refer to syllables or sounds—i.e. it is phonetic rather than hieroglyphic, like the Egyptian alphabet, which operates with ideograms. That said, letters such as Kaph, Ayin (a circle like O) and Aleph had their origins in images of hand, eye and ox's head respectively. The word 'alphabet' itself comes from Alphabetha, a juxtaposition of Latin letters which originate in the Phoenician Aleph and Beth.

For Romanos Iliya, it was less the aesthetic appeal of Phoenician that drew her to study the alphabet and make sculptures based on the letters, more a sense of the power of the language itself, and how that tied in with her own quest for identity.

As she puts it, 'The simplicity of the alphabet not only allowed it to be used by multiple languages, but impacted communication within the coastal cities that came in contact with Phoenicians. Disappointed that such an important achievement, part of our Lebanese heritage, was so underrated, I felt I was on a mission to put it in the limelight.'

Initially she worked on two-dimensional representations of the letters, but then gradually let them evolve into three-dimensional forms that she translated into bronze sculptures. The resulting works, while immediately recognisable as the original letters, also contain layers of meaning, relating to past and present. She placed sculptures of individual letters in relation to each other, adding another layer of meaning. Romanos Iliya playfully refers to these as 'scrabble', as she created words in both Arabic and English. The sculptures, cast in bronze—the metal used by Phoenicians—and mounted on plinths of layered plywood, convey an immediate message of strength and endurance. The layered wood also suggests the passage of time. The plywood has, as its top layer, a sheet of mirrored stainless steel, representing the importance of the Mediterranean to this ancient seafaring people. In one sculpture, *Alphabeit*, the letter Aleph appears to be walking towards the letter Beth, the latter meaning 'home' in both ancient Phoenician and in modern Arabic ('Beit').

These are works clearly created within contemporary modes of representation and abstraction, but they also celebrate the cultural heritage of Lebanon. However, in no way does this lessen their universal appeal, and Romanos Iliya's sculptures are equally at home in New York or London, as much as in Beirut. Indeed, many of her works have been acquired for collections outside of Lebanon, in France, Britain and the United States, as well as in the Arab world.

Born in Lebanon, Romanos Iliya was one of the million or so civilians whose lives were affected by the bloody civil war of 1975–1990; but, unlike many, her family chose not to flee the country. For this, they paid a heavy price, losing family members, experiencing disruption and trauma. After attending French school, she went on to complete a degree in architecture at the American University in Beirut, before travelling to France where she studied design at ADAC in Paris.

While based there, she used the opportunity to travel widely, before moving back to her home country, which, back then, was well on its way to recovering from the civil war and becoming again a lively centre for business and culture. In Beirut, she worked on the reconstruction of buildings in the Central District, while also completing other architectural and design projects in Lebanon.

In 2001, Romanos Iliya moved to London, and a few years later to Hong Kong. During this period, she continued to expand her range of interests and knowledge, immersing herself in the arts and culture of the countries she had the opportunity to visit and, while living in Hong Kong, completing a diploma course in Feng Shui with the renowned tutor Chow Hon-Ming.

Returning to the Middle East, to live in Dubai, she took sculpture classes and became immediately passionate about it, starting sculpting on a full-time basis. It was her first time living in an Arab country outside her native Lebanon, and being exposed to an Arab culture different from hers. She started questioning her own identity, looking back in history, and delving into the world of the Phoenicians and their ancient alphabet—perhaps their most tangible and enduring contribution to world culture. She created her first series of sculptures based on this fascination with the ancient symbols.

The sculptures she creates are personal, made in the consciousness that their form has to convey an intrinsic, emotional, meaning. When working as an architect, Romanos Iliya designed with an understanding of how function determines the form of an object. Now, liberated from this constraint, she makes sculptures whose function is to speak to the sense of aesthetic beauty, and also to the artist's own subconscious, as she weaves together past and present, and re-evaluates her own preconceptions and feelings regarding her native country. She has also played with the forms of modernist concrete poetry, fusing together words in different fonts and sizes, creating abstract images that are in fact composed of individual words, each one of which summons to mind an image. The words 'identity', 'barrier' and 'boundaries' are writ large, while 'self-esteem', 'emotion' and 'happiness' are in tiny letters. This is an art that actively engages the viewer, provoking thought and reflection on how meaning is formed, in a subtle and intelligent way.

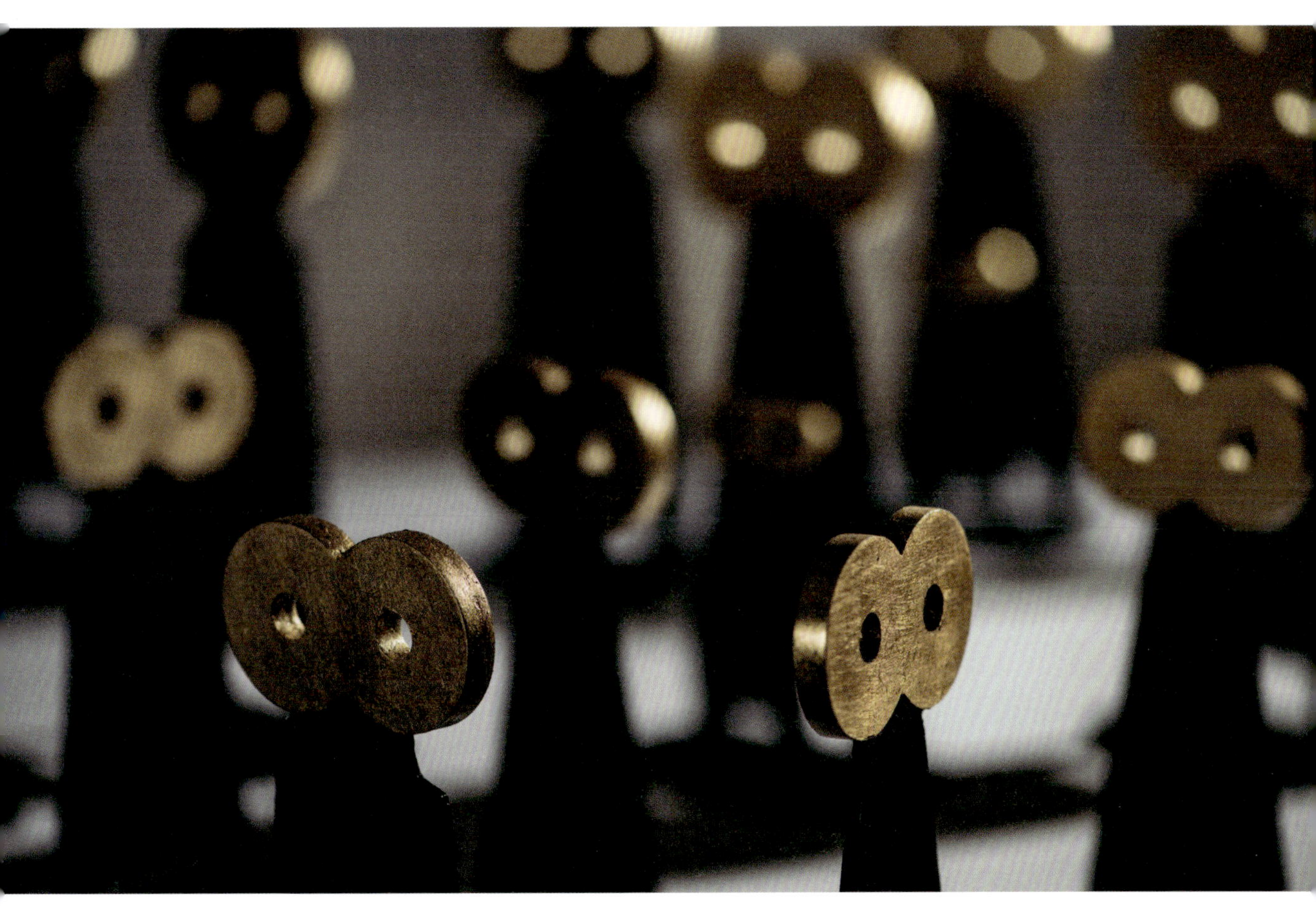

EYE IDOLS, 2015

Romanos Iliya creates sculptures on radically different scales; as well as large, outdoor pieces, there are small works, suitable for domestic houses. Cast in resin in limited editions, they are sold through the National Museum of Beirut and the AUB Archaeology Museum. Some of Romanos Iliya's sculptures can even be worn as jewellery. Her *Eye Idols* are small and simple in form: black, schematic torsos surmounted by two gold circles, representing eyes. These *Eye Idols* are based on votive figurines found in an ancient temple discovered in the 1930s by archaeologist Max Mallowan, at Tell Brak, in the north-east of Syria. Romanos Iliya was drawn to the remarkably modern appearance of these simple but powerful figurines. Sadly, the site of Tell Brak has been looted during the ongoing civil war in Syria, and the artist's symbolic figurines bear silent witness to the destruction of this ancient city site.

Also small in scale, her silver and brass spirals, made in collaboration with jeweller Randa Tabbah and shown at Beirut Design Week in 2016, can be worn as bracelets. These works are in fact double spirals, one of which is designed to be worn as a bracelet, while the other remains fixed to a small plinth, which bears inscriptions on its four sides: 'The Whirlpool of Water', 'The Path of the Earth', 'The Lift of the Wind' and 'The Spin of a Galaxy'.

Whether large or small, Romanos Iliya's sculptures are works of art that operate in complex, multi-layered ways, in the everyday world, in art galleries, and also in the context of Beirut Art Week, where she exhibits annually.

Romanos Iliya is equally at home working in an urban context. A few months after she moved back to Lebanon in 2013, she showcased 'Alphabeit' (p. 88) in downtown Beirut as part of the first edition of Beirut Art Week. This initiative encouraged people to explore the urban landscape of the capital through a tour featuring art installations and sculptures: 'It became a yearly rendezvous, as I loved the way art lovers and passers-by alike interacted with my work, and I was very much interested to experiment with scale.' Romanos Iliya's public art works include several located in Beirut. Standing in a stylish shopping centre in the centre of the old souk district, *Entangled Love* (pp. 86–87), made of brass and stainless steel, seems at first glance to be an abstract work, with vestigial hands reaching out to touch, and curves and rounded forms suggesting an organic familial situation; the forms are in fact individual letters, L, O, V, E.

Her sculpture *Noughts and Crosses* (p. 91) was exhibited during the 2014 Beirut Art Week. In this work, the letters Taw, like an X, and Ayin, resembling a circle, are combined: Taw meaning 'sign', while Ayin signifies the eye. In *TRAP* (p. 77), the letters Taw and Peh, resembling the cross and crescent, are set in a wire cage—a reference both to centuries of religious conflict, and the manner in which people become trapped in their own histories and identities. In *Comme un poisson dans l'eau* (2012) (pp. 82–83), also made of brass and polished stainless steel, two letters of the Phoenician alphabet, Mêm (water) and Nun (fish), interact on a mirrored surface representing the sea. In 2017, her sculpture *Live-Life* (pp. 58–59), a series of four bronze forms representing the words 'Live' and 'Life', was the centrepiece of a fundraising event in London by the charity LIFE; that same year, a large sculpture, *Hobb* (p. 62) was displayed in an open-air setting in Beirut Central District.

Although she became more a full-time sculptor in 2011, Romanos Iliya continues to work in a multi-disciplinary way, combining design, architecture and sculpture in various media, always showing a definite flair and sense of assurance. In addition to having her own work exhibited in Dubai and Beirut, she has curated exhibitions, including one featuring Lebanese designers, held at Salon du Meuble in Paris. Combining these roles is essential in Beirut, a city hoping, in spite of many difficulties and catastrophes, to achieve its old pre-eminence in the Eastern Mediterranean as a centre for art, design and culture. These often-tragic events have informed Romanos Iliya's art.

In the *Flower Power* series (2019), the starting point of each sculpture was a found object relating to the Lebanese civil war. Three large-scale works evoking flowers, fans or peacock feathers, but also made from discarded armaments, were shown in downtown Beirut, while an installation of smaller works, incorporating rocket and bomb casings, was on show at the Abroyan factory. She describes the process of making these works as 'therapeutic, aiming to engage, raise awareness, and address issues of memory and sustainability, while conveying, at the same time, an unostentatious yet powerful message of love, peace and hope.'

Romanos Iliya has not returned to her native country with naïve preconceptions. She has used her sculpture, and the study of the history of Lebanon, to indicate a pathway towards the future, one in which peaceful co-existence is possible. She has also, through art, and the Phoenician alphabet, rediscovered her own pride in her nationality and patrimony. Those lucky enough to have lived in Beirut, or visited the city, in the decades before 1975, remember it as one of the most vibrant places in existence. Romanos Iliya is playing a key role in highlighting her cultural legacy and restoring its historical contribution to the world.

PETER MURRAY, 2019

Sir Peter Murray CBE founded the award-winning Yorkshire Sculpture Park in 1977, and has been developing the project ever since. The first and finest of its kind, it is renowned in the UK and internationally.

INSTALLATION OF **FLOWER POWER** SERIES AT ABROYAN FACTORY, BORJ HAMMOUD, 2019

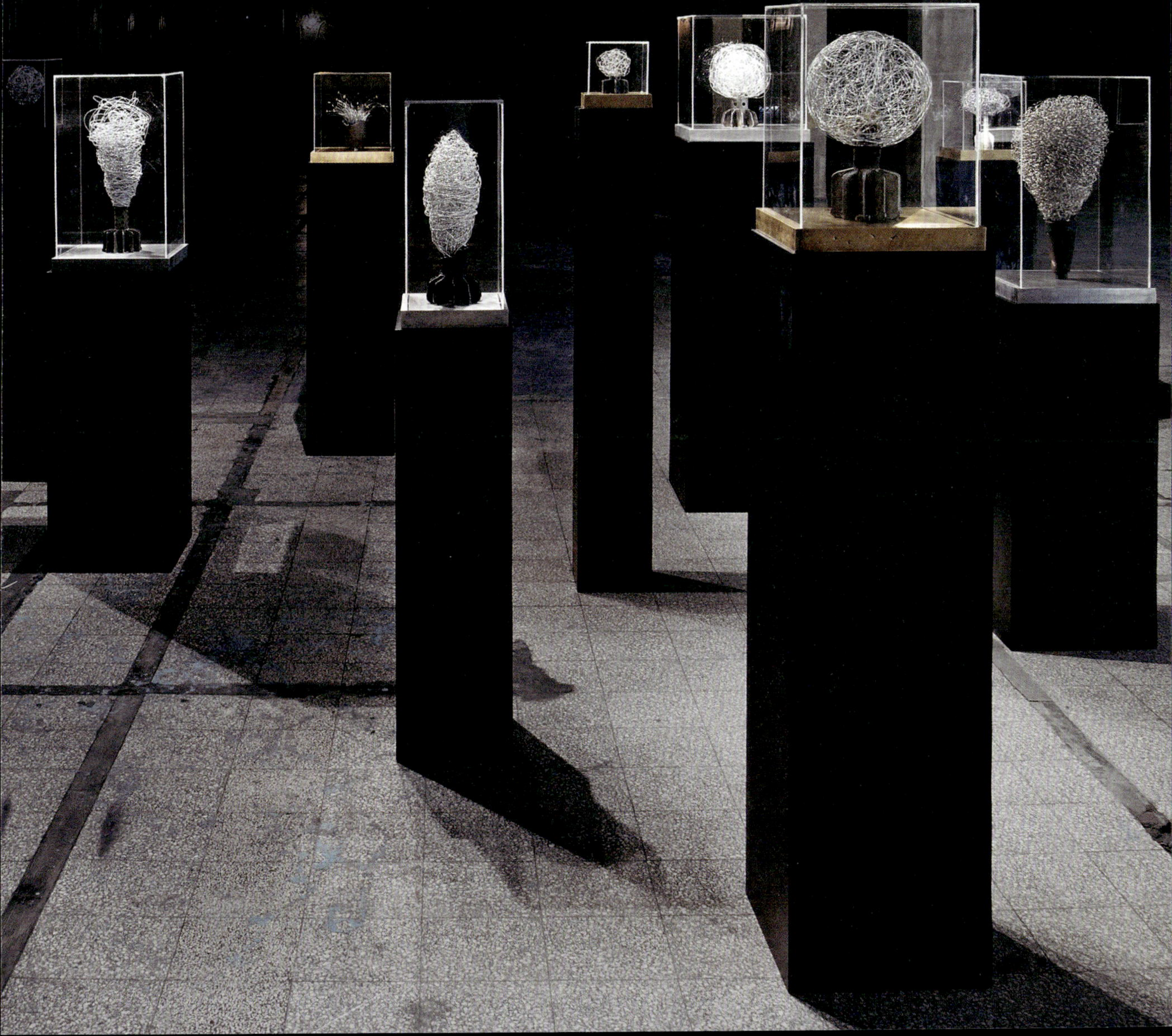

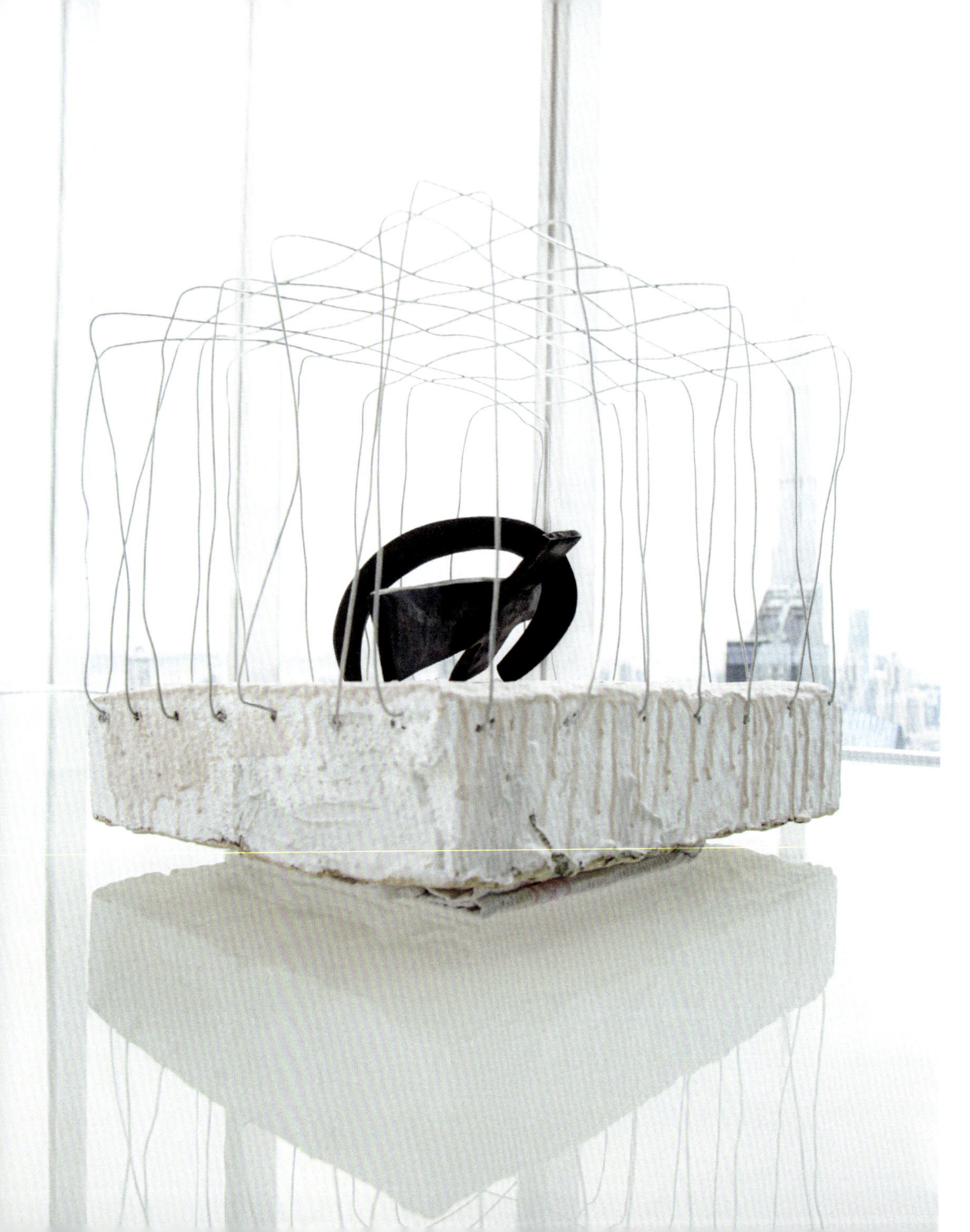

You were born in Lebanon before the 1975 'civil war', when different factions were heavily armed; you experienced the effects of that conflict at first hand. Having seen so much destruction, what made you decide to study architecture?

I was thirteen when the Lebanese civil war started. My parents, unlike many of their friends, chose not to flee the country. They tried their best to protect me and my siblings in the face of tragedies, but enduring years of bloody conflict cannot but leave indelible traces. Changing schools and frequent internal displacements were dictated by security issues, not to mention periods of mere survival, when real, active life was at a standstill. In 1976, I lost a cousin, an only child killed in front of his parents, who were both seriously injured, during the Damour massacre.[1] A few years later, in 1982, my aunt was assassinated at close range in a street of the capital; we never found out who killed her and why.

I enrolled, like other members of my family, as a volunteer at the Lebanese Red Cross, and was actively involved in humanitarian and social activities from the beginning of the civil war up until college in 1979. This was very taxing at times, but always rewarding.

As a child, I liked drawing and building structures with Lego, so I had no hesitation in applying for architecture at the American University of Beirut. Back then, and in spite of the war, it was the best college in the region, and I loved the fact that students were very mixed: all walks of life, all religions, all political affiliations. Its campus was located in West Beirut, while we lived on the other side of the 'Green Line', and I sometimes couldn't go home for weeks because it was dangerous to cross the demarcation zone separating Christian and Muslim factions in East and West Beirut respectively.

Beirut, back then, had a crazy energy—we took risks to 'live' as normally as possible, although it was in fact surreal. Adrenaline kicked in, and partying few blocks away from snipers, as the neighbourhood was being shelled, was 'normal'! It was during this period that I experienced, par excellence, the dichotomy of the Lebanese people: resilient and free spirited, seldom looking back. We have the impressive capacity to absorb hardships and yet we rarely confront the causes of them. Hence, sadly, we do not learn from them.

Starting a career as an architect surrounded by destruction, in a country torn apart by war, seemed ironic. But, as the events unfolded over time, some areas of Lebanon remained relatively safe, even flourishing at the expense of other regions due to internal displacement, which made it possible to work in spite of the ever-challenging conditions.

How easy was it to travel from Lebanon to elsewhere before you moved to Paris? There you took part in the design workshops at ADAC (now Paris-Ateliers). In what way did that experience change your artistic direction?

Travelling was difficult, but I managed to make one or two trips a year, to discover the world little by little, and to live, if only for a moment, another reality. I had planned to spend August 1989 between the United States and France. Beirut airport was closed; to leave the country, I had to take a Cyprus-bound hydrofoil from Jounieh,[2] a coastal city north of the capital. Departures were scheduled at night as, at the time, Syrian gunners bombarded the enclave's coastline regularly to prevent supplies of weapons and fuel from reaching the Christians.

Waiting to embark, I met a friend who was there with her husband and their two baby girls. We agreed to catch up on board later. I had just arrived on the boat's deck when a salvo of shells targeted the bay, forcing the hydrofoil to depart abruptly, leaving some passengers and suitcases behind. After a lull, a small boat ferried them, but another battery of rockets was fired. The boat capsized. A surreal, apocalyptic scene was to follow. Our hydrofoil picked up some of the passengers, among them my friend, while others, including her husband, were rescued and taken back ashore. The tragedy resulted in the death of the two baby girls, who were found drowned the next day. This trauma stayed for many years in our hearts and minds.

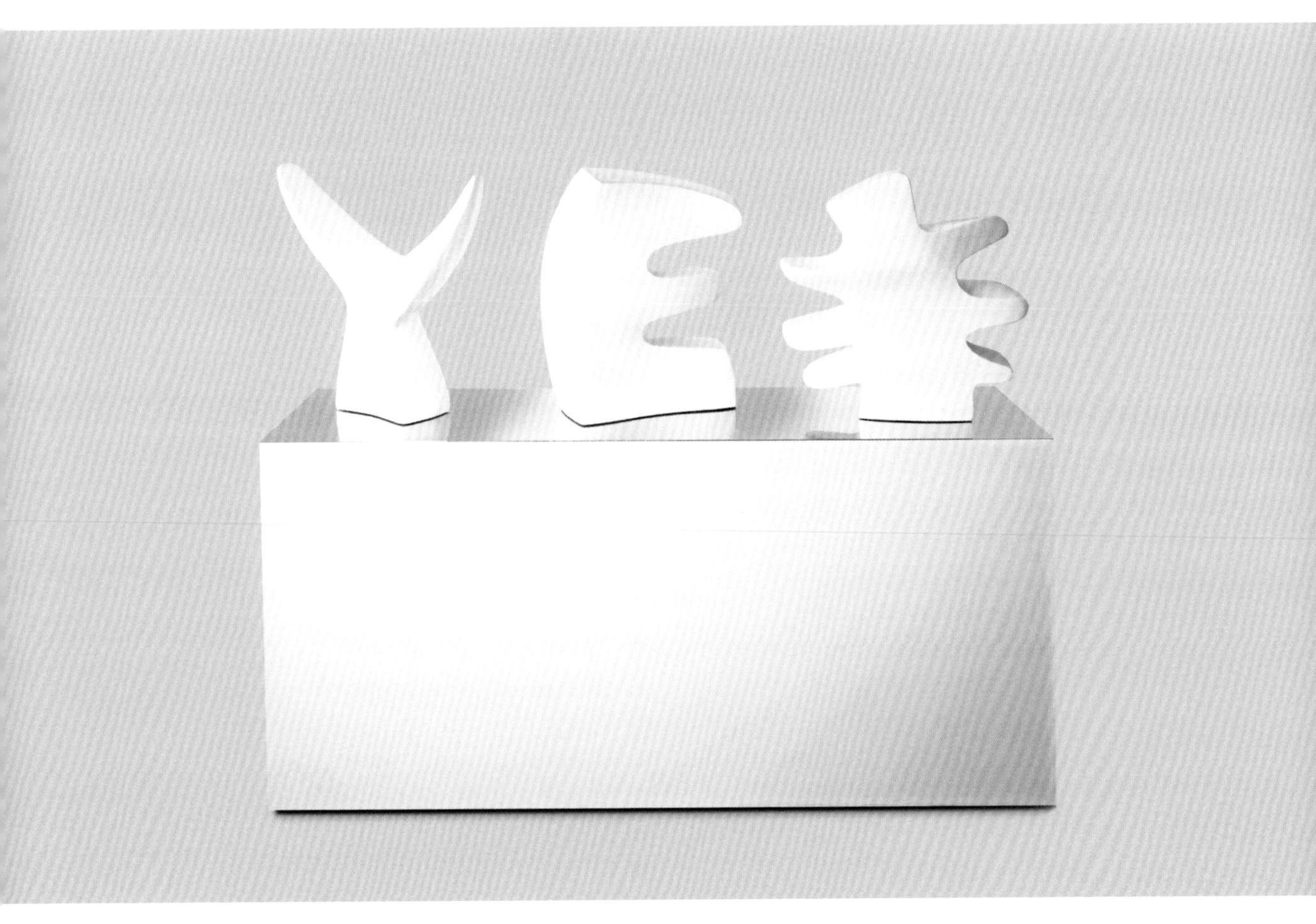

ABOVE: **YES**, RESIN, MIRRORED STAINLESS STEEL, WOOD. 142 X 160 X 40 CM, 2017
PREVIOUS PAGE: **TRAP**, BRONZE, GALVANIZED WIRE, POLYSTYRENE AND RESIN, 29 X 32 X 29 CM, 2012

Paris, where I moved a few months later, was a new chapter in my life. I wanted to make up for lost time, and made the most of what the city had to offer, especially its cultural and artistic wealth. I pursued design workshops at ADAC, building my own prototypes. I learned a lot from this hands-on approach, and enjoyed the tactile aspect of creation. Frequent trips to Milan, among other destinations, further enhanced my interest in design.

In the meantime, the Lebanese civil war came to an end, and rebuilding the country was on the agenda. I returned home in 1993, hopeful, and excited to be part of that reconstruction. I started working as a freelancer, then built a small team around me. Most of my projects were renovations of old buildings in downtown Beirut, as well as the interior design of varied commercial and residential projects in Lebanon.

For over a decade you travelled, and lived in cities quite different from each other, moving from Paris, Hong Kong, to Dubai and London. What triggered your move from architecture and design to become a sculptor and visual artist?

I always follow my heart. All my moves were triggered by my personal life; my husband's career gave us the chance to live in different parts of the world.

First came London in 2001, then Hong Kong a few years later, and our final long stay abroad was Dubai, from 2010 to 2013. While this did not necessarily suit my profession as an architect, I embraced every single experience. Besides travelling extensively, discovering new places and absorbing their cultural and artistic heritage, I seized opportunities to broaden up my spectrum of interests around architecture, namely design, Feng Shui and, last but not least, art.

Dubai was a different experience. The city, although welcoming and easy to live in except for during its hot season, did not offer the cultural and artistic richness of the places I had lived in before. My interest in art had grown substantially over the years, as I spent a lot of time visiting museums, going to art exhibitions and other artistic events. However, Dubai turned out it to be a blessing in disguise!

It was a pivotal time in my life; I felt the need to pause and reflect, to introspect, and to find myself. It was in this context that I discovered my passion for sculpture, after enrolling in a first workshop, then another, then starting sculpting at home as I became instantly passionate about it. The icing on the cake was 'Tashkeel',[3] a unique art facility in the UAE. I was lucky to get hold of a work space there, benefiting from the multi-disciplinary studios, workshops and other amenities. This allowed me to grow my new creative practice in a stimulating environment that encouraged dialogue among practitioners, and I was delighted to show my work for the first time with them in Bastakiya. This changed the direction of my life, giving me the incentive to invest myself; I never felt so good.

What stimulated you to create the Phoenician alphabet series?

After spending many years in different parts of the world, coupled with constant back-and-forth trips to Lebanon, living in Dubai was my first experience of living in another Arab country and being exposed to an Arab culture that is different from mine. I started reflecting on my own identity.

I love Lebanese-French author Amin Maalouf, and *Les Identités Meurtrières*[4] is a book I read thoroughly around that period. Moving across the world's history, faiths and politics, Maalouf advocates that, in the age of globalisation, we need to live our multiple identities and recognise our uniqueness, rather than feel forced to choose between excessive assertion and the loss of identity altogether.

I remember a discussion with my husband, asking if, as a Lebanese, he felt more Arab or Phoenician. He answered: 'Phoenician, of course, because I have been exporting myself to the world since age twenty.' His answer triggered a quest: I immersed myself in the Phoenician civilisation and history. Driven by their desire for trade, the Phoenicians sailed far and wide, were credited with many important nautical inventions, and firmly established a reputation as masters of the sea. But their greatest legacy and enduring contribution to humanity, it seemed to me, was their alphabet. The more I delved into it, the more it fascinated me.

The Phoenician alphabet was written from right to left; it is an *abjad*[5] of twenty-two consonants only, which was a radical simplification of phonetic writing. Its ease of use compared with other languages at the time meant one could quickly learn how to read and write it. Also, the maritime trading culture of Phoenician merchants made it spread fast, especially as they established coastal cities, including Carthage, Sicily, Corsica, Malta and Sardinia. Over time, the Phoenician alphabet gave rise to a number of writing systems, including Greek and Aramaic, which in turn evolved into alphabets, such as Latin, Cyrillic or Arabic, among the most widely used in the world today.

I was delighted to know that this great contribution to the world was recognised by UNESCO as a Lebanese heritage, and disappointed to realise that, back home, it was not highlighted as such.

The Phoenician Alphabet series was my first body of work: creating sculptures inspired by the letters happened spontaneously, as I felt I was on a mission to give a new life to these archaic symbols. The process was therapeutic. It rekindled my relationship with my home country at a time when I had conflicting emotions towards it, helping me to reconcile the present while paying tribute to the past.

To what extent are the letters and words that inspired your sculptures important to you? And which words stand out as the most essential?

Calligraphy, in particular Arabic and Chinese, intrigues me. But it was not only the appeal of the Phoenician symbols that drew me to create this series. It was the power behind the alphabet. Its impact as it spread, and how quickly it transformed communication back then, fuelled my imagination, as well as the urge for self-exploration. I started sculpting figures influenced by each of the twenty-two Phoenician letters, over and over again. I was in trance. The shapes, meanings and symbolism of the letters fascinated me and, through them, I envisaged glimpses into the past that I translated freely in my forms.

The Phoenician letters were named after animals, parts of the human body, or daily life activities, and their corresponding symbol was a schematic drawing of

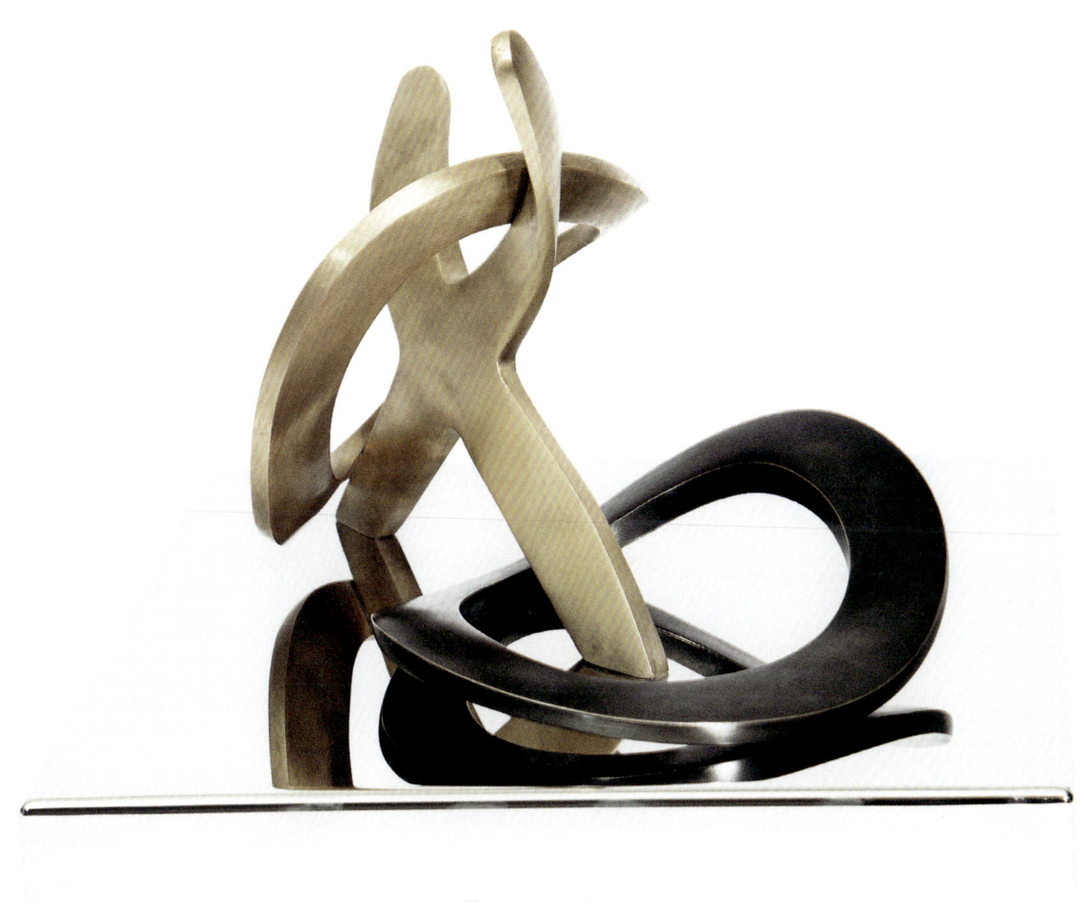

TIC TAC TOE, BRONZE, MIRRORED STAINLESS STEEL 19 X 25 X 25 CM, 2019

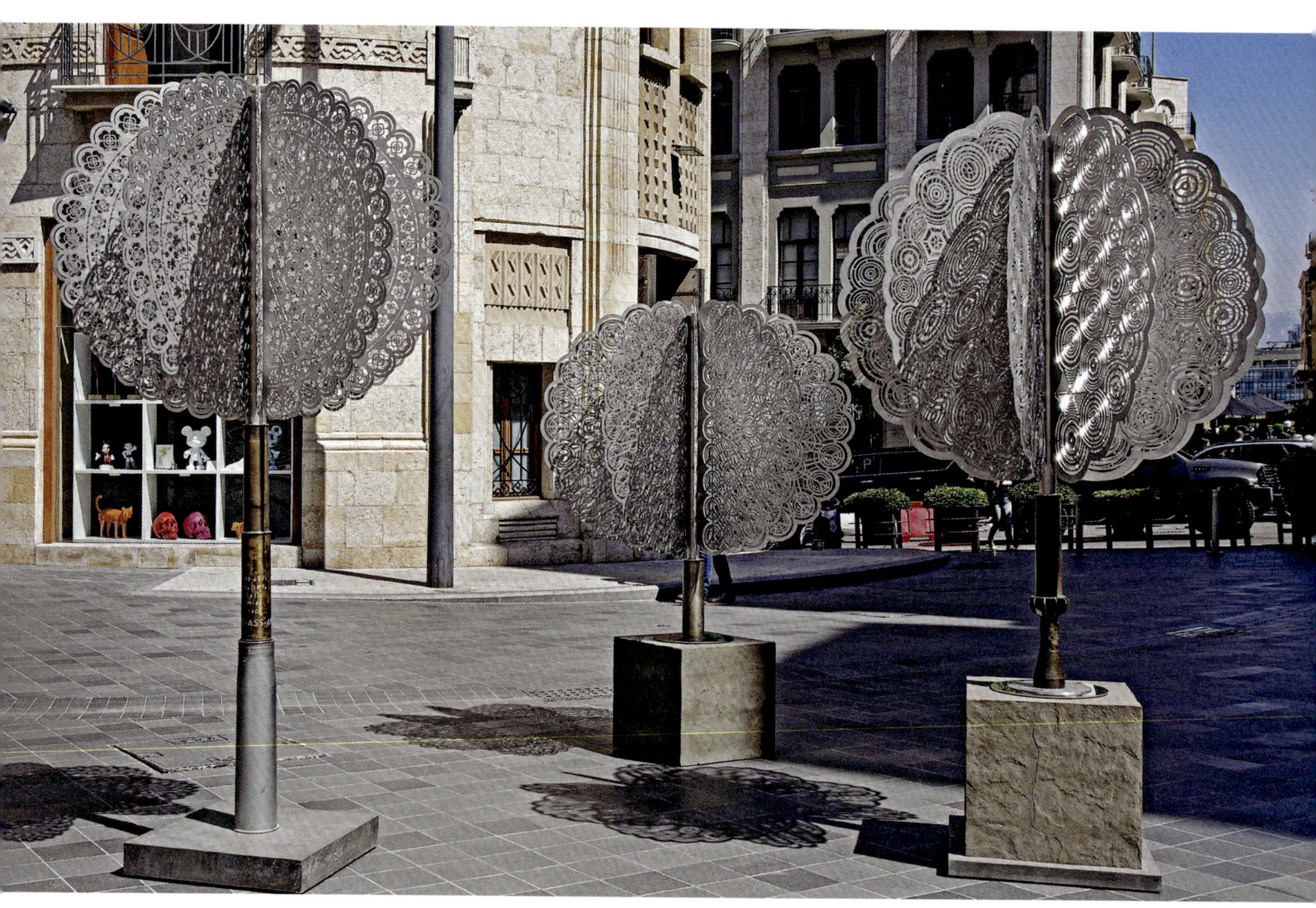

INSTALLATION OF **FLOWER POWER** SERIES IN DOWNTOWN BEIRUT, 2019

such words. Some of them had universal shapes like a circle or a cross, and they all looked modern, yet they were ancient.

I refer to these first sculptures as *Characters & Letters*. To me, creating them was an act of revival as I felt the letters were being transformed into personas, with different characters and presence, whether small or large.

The first figures were done in plaster or clay, allowing flexibility and ease of manipulation. I sculpted several versions for each letter and, clearly, they evolved from early forms that were relatively flat to more and more three-dimensional. I carried the models to Beirut and cast my first batch there. They had to be in bronze, the metal used by Phoenicians. I wanted to learn about the casting process, and experiment with different finishings.

The first prototypes of the small works were made of solid bronze scraps. The resulting sculptures were heavy, and had patches of varied hues and textures that conveyed beautifully the passage of time. In other editions, I experimented casting with other metals such as aluminium, brass, stainless steel, as well as resin. It was intriguing to perceive how different materials and textures affect our perception of the same form, be it in the way it catches light, the energy it exudes, or how it changes our relationship to the space around it.

The sculptures evolved as I placed individual letters in relation to each other, hence adding another layer of meaning and creating words. I called that series *Scrabble & Word*, in reference to the game we used to play in the shelters during the civil war.

The choice of materials was important. All the figures are cast in bronze, and mounted on plinths of layered plywood, both intrinsic parts of the work. The plywood has as its top layer a sheet of mirrored stainless steel—symbol for water, a vital element to this ancient seafaring people. This assemblage gives a sense of endurance and suggests the passage of time.

The first work from this series was *OK-KO* (p. 62), chosen because OK is the most spoken word on the planet, used even by people who don't speak English.

I was thrilled that both Latin letters O and K have exactly the same shape as the Phoenician letters *Ayin*[6] and *Kaph*,[7] which illustrates the alphabet's evolution. As the Phoenician alphabet was read from right to left, I found it amusing to note that if one were to 'read' the sculpture from left to right—in Latin—it would be 'OK', while right to left—in Phoenician—would be 'KO'.

And then came other words that carry universal (mostly positive) emotions and concepts, ones that had a pivotal importance in my life, such as *Love, Hope, Live-Life* and *Peace*, as well as names of cities dear to me, starting with *Beirut*, but also *Paris, HK* or *Dubai* (pp. 64–69).

To me, the most essential word is hope. It is a powerful word, and a much-needed one.

You moved from letters to words and then to scripts and monograms, experimenting with scale, compositions and materials. How did the aesthetic vision impose itself on you?

In the *Scripts & Monogram* series, letters, combined for their meanings, symbols or forms, fuse poetry and verbal significance to depict stories, portray idioms, and express concerns that are close to my heart.

As in the *Scrabble & Words* series, specific materials and finishings, used for their symbolic value, are an inherent part of the process. This is the case for both figures and the plinth supporting them, as they are indissociable elements of the work.

Love is everywhere (p. 78) illustrates the intrinsic role of the mirrored steel base. Boundaries between sculpture and support are blurred as the plinth reflects the curves of *Lamed* (character representing letter L), portraying an overall image of intermingling heart shapes.

Manipulating scale plays an important role too. In *Alphabeit* (pp. 88–89), I contrasted the size and the medium of letters *Aleph* and *Beth*, their juxtaposition being the origin of the word 'alphabet'. *Beth*, the meaning of which is 'house', just as in Arabic, was rotated and oversized, and put in relation with *Aleph*, the silhouette of which reminds me of a human figure. As it is the first letter of the alphabet, I often use it as a main character in my narratives. It is also the case in *The Black Sheep* (p. 79), in which the finish of the sculptures is key: several representations of the same figure are used in contrasting shiny gold and oxidised black.

In Trap (p. 77), I was inspired by Maalouf's book (see note 4), highlighting how the religious layer of our identity can overshadow all others. Two decades after the end of the civil war, most Lebanese are still stuck—consciously or not—in their religious ghettos.

Hobb (p. 62), the Arabic word for love, portrays an abstract image that is in fact the interaction of the two Phoenician letters *Heth* and *Beth* that compose the word 'hobb'. Meaning respectively 'wall' and 'house', they are in cold-cast bronze and stand on a solid concrete base. This work exemplifies how composition, meanings and material all contribute to add layers of interpretation, weaving together the present and the past.

After your Phoenician alphabet, your recent public art installations, more abstract, have their narratives linked to recent events in Lebanon.

After decades of intermittent war, returning home brought its share of challenges and contradictory feelings: burying memories, ignoring traces. *Flower Power* became my next body of work. The starting point of the sculptures is a war-related found object, the base, to which I added symbolic elements such as flowers, trees and hearts to give it a poetic language. The choice of materials highlights the dichotomy between war and peace, shells and flowers. My concern was in terms of memory and sustainability, as the country was literally drowning in its own waste, the tip of Lebanese corruption, irresponsibility and inadequacy.

My latest work—a public art installation, *On the Other Side of Time*—was finally unveiled in 2021, after the devastating explosion in Beirut, August 2020. Located in a prominent crossroad of the capital it is inspired by Dante's *Divina Commedia*, its themes of hell, purgatory and paradise—an apt allegory of man's journey through life towards salvation. The deep-rooted symbolism of the theme is acutely pertinent in Lebanon, where decades of negligence, corruption and impunity have tested both individual and social consciousness to their limits. This was my answer to the time and place, a comedy turned into tragedy; and while 'Paradise' seems a long way ahead, the art aims at instilling some belief that there exists, still, a ray of hope.

Dealing with most aspects of daily life in Lebanon is beyond frustrating, but what I saw was just the tip of the iceberg. I had to translate the anger, which conflicted with the sweetness of home and its humanity, into a form of creativity in order to survive. This love and hate relationship with my country will be, forever, a blessing and a curse.

LONDON, JUNE 2022

[1] Damour is a Lebanese Christian town 20 km south of Beirut. The name of the town is derived from the name of the Phoenician god Damoros, who symbolised immortality. The Damour massacres during the Lebanese civil war of 1975–1990 took place in January 1976. More than 150,000 people died in Lebanon's fifteen-year war. Half a million of Lebanese were displaced, most of them deliberately driven from their homes by militiamen of rival religious clans.

[2] Jounieh is a coastal city between Beirut and Byblos. During the civil war, Beirut was divided into East and West and, as violence escalated, many Christians fled to safer areas. Jounieh witnessed a massive migration.

[3] Tashkeel, established in 2008, is a contemporary art centre featuring work studios for a variety of media, plus exhibitions and classes. It still provides a nurturing environment for the growth of contemporary art and design practice.

[4] Amin Maalouf, *In the Name of Identity: Violence and the Need to Belong*, Penguin, 1998.

[5] The name 'abjad' is derived from pronouncing the first letters of the Arabic alphabet order; this ordering matches that of the older Phoenician proto-alphabet. It is a writing system in which only consonants are represented, leaving vowels sounds to be inferred by the reader.

[6] The Phoenician letter *Ayin* means eye; in Arabic *Eyn* has the same meaning, but could also mean source/spring

[7] The Phoenician letter *Kaph* means the palm of the hand; in Arabic *Kaf* has the same meaning..

ROSE ISSA AND NAYLA ROMANOS ILIYA IN FRONT OF **ON THE OTHER SIDE OF TIME**, BEIRUT, 2020

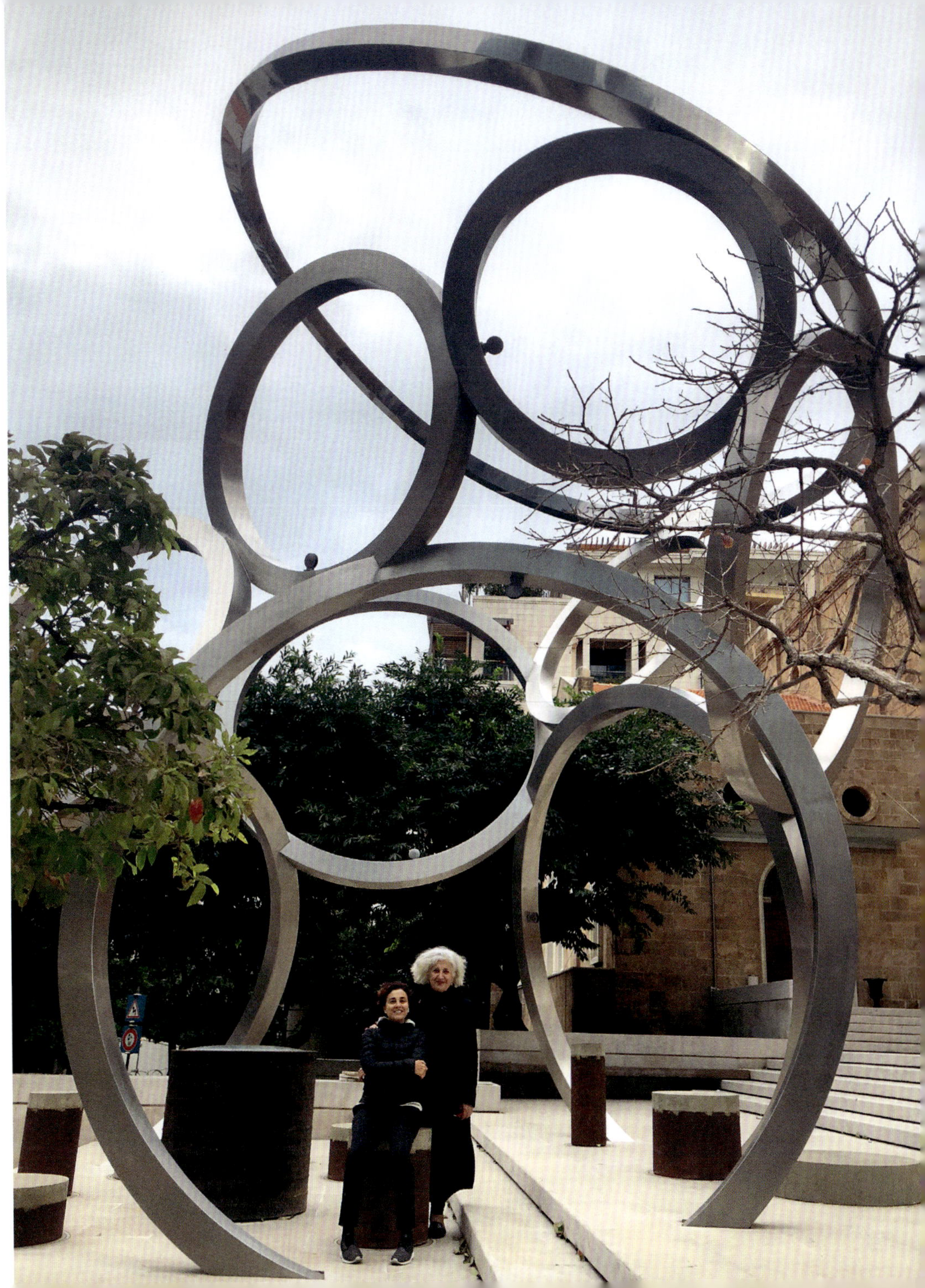

CHARACTERS | LETTERS

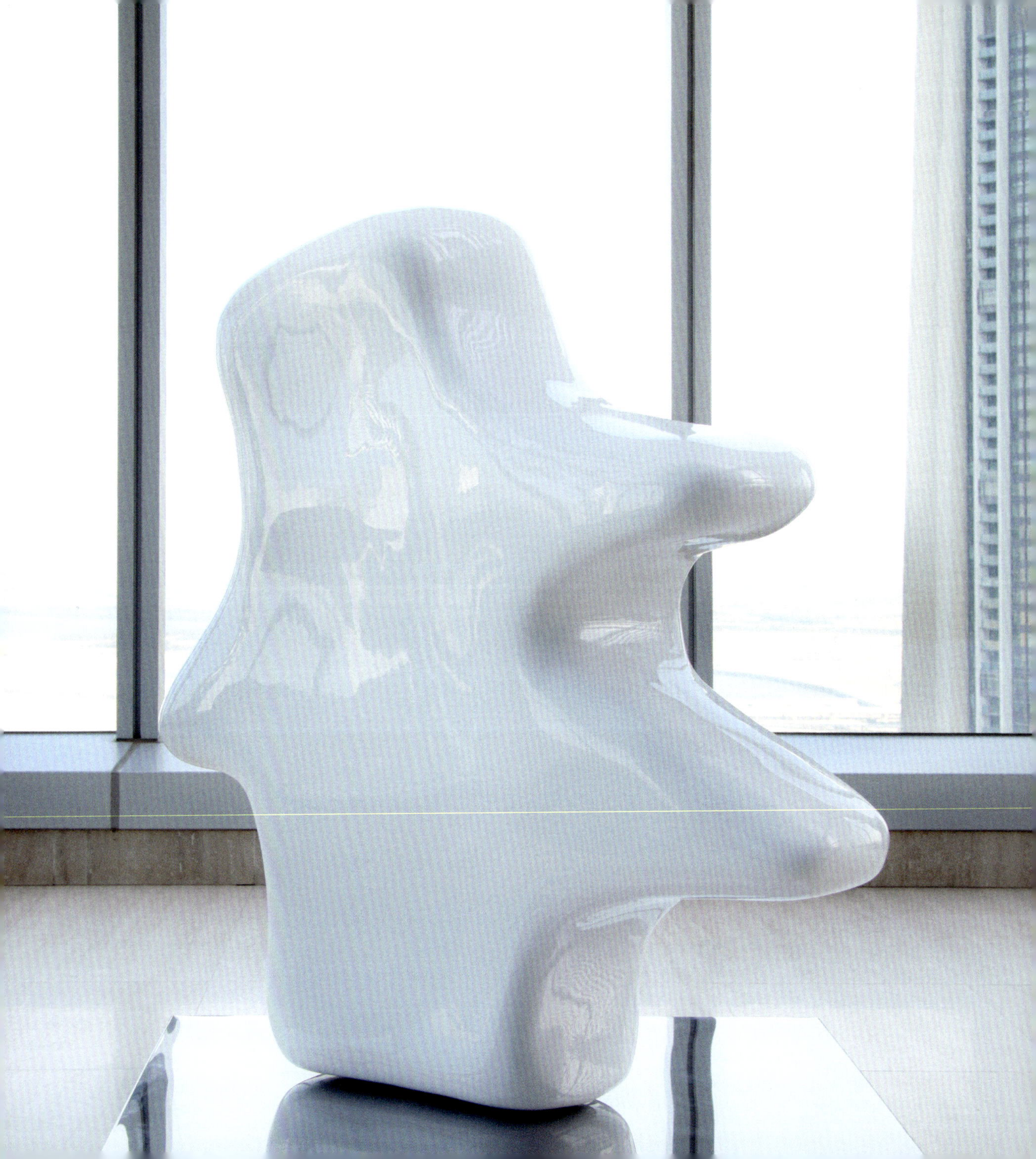

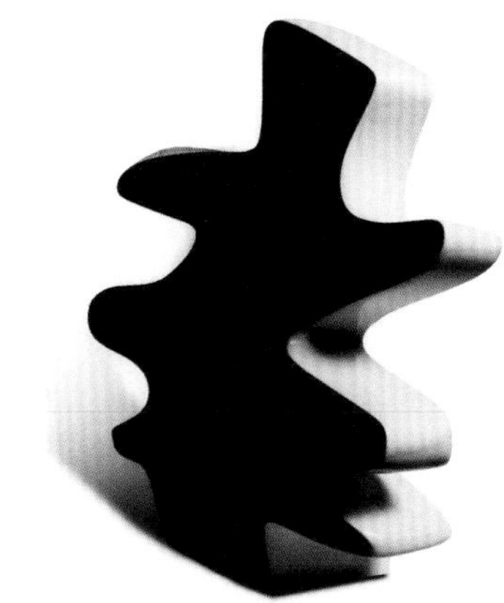

ABOVE: **SAMEK**, GLASS FIBRE AND RESIN, AUTOMOTIVE PAINT, 58 X 55 X 16 CM, 2016
LEFT: **ALEPH**, GLASS FIBRE AND RESIN, MIRRORED STAINLESS STEEL, 145 X 110 X 110 CM, 2012

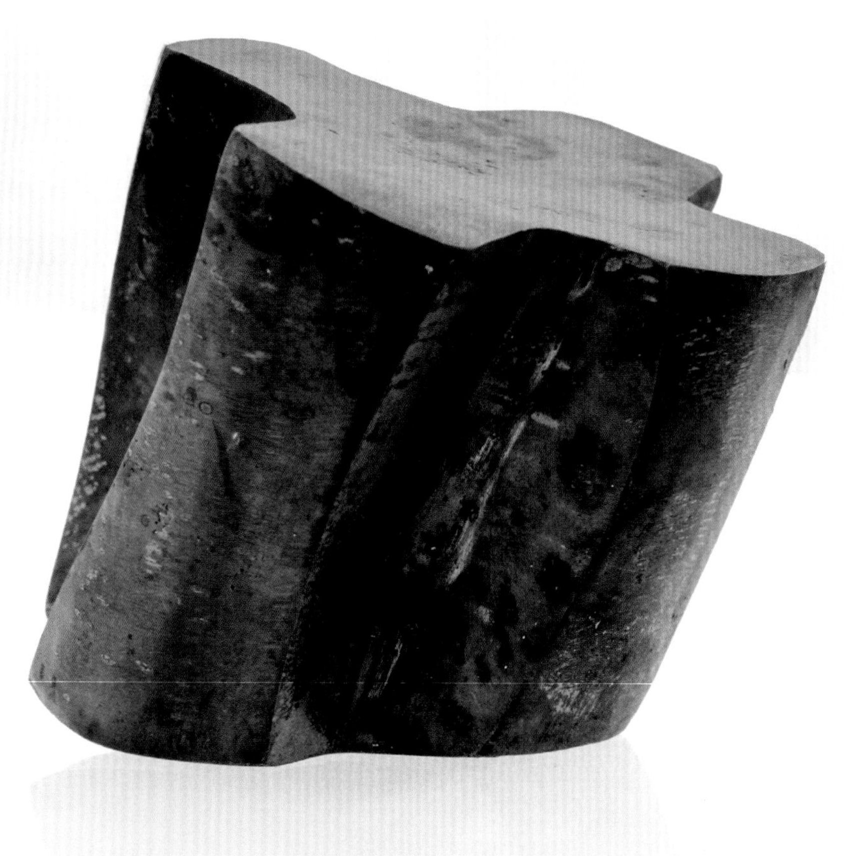

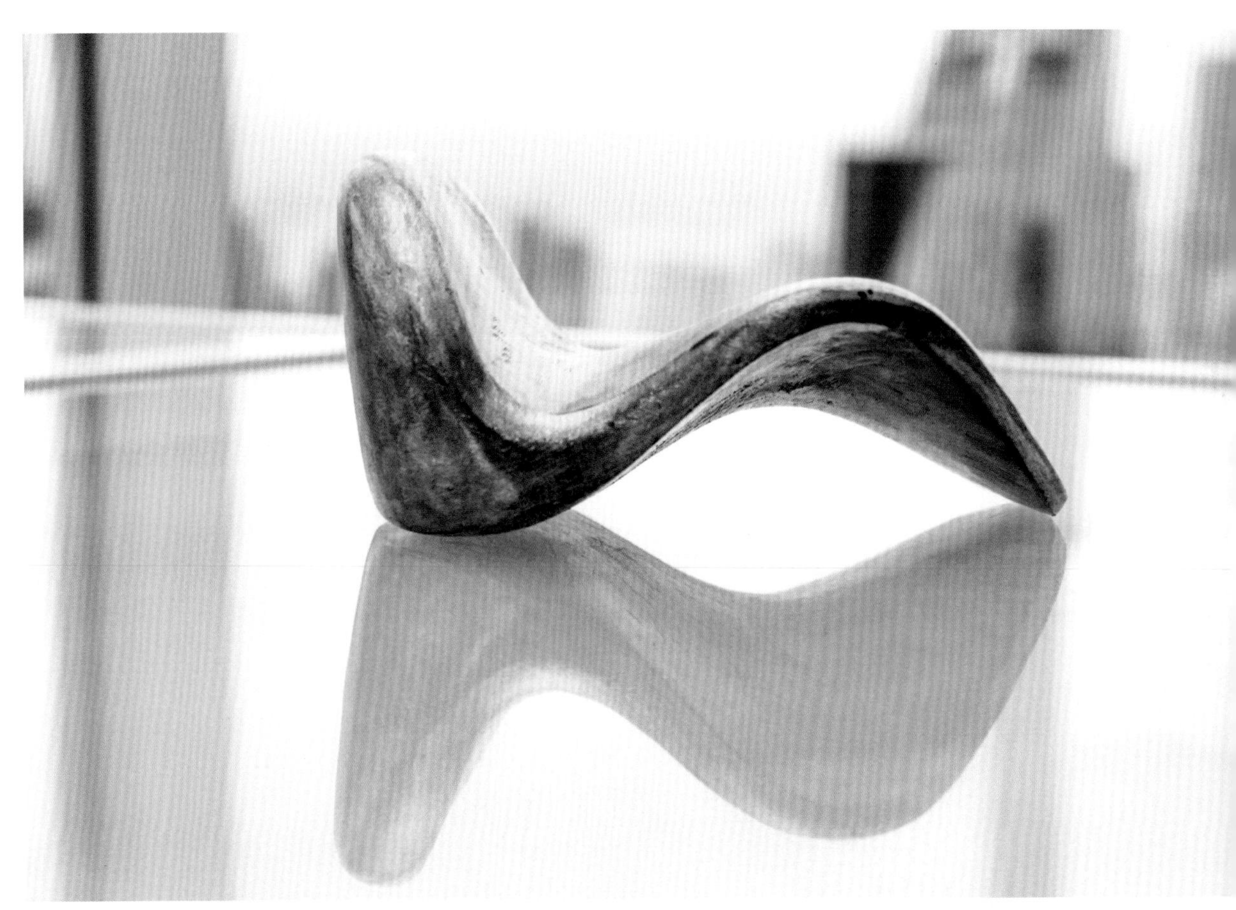

LEFT: **TETH**, BRONZE, 12 X 10 X 10 CM, 2013, ABOVE: **NUN**, ALUMINIUM, 12 X 22 X 16 CM, 2012

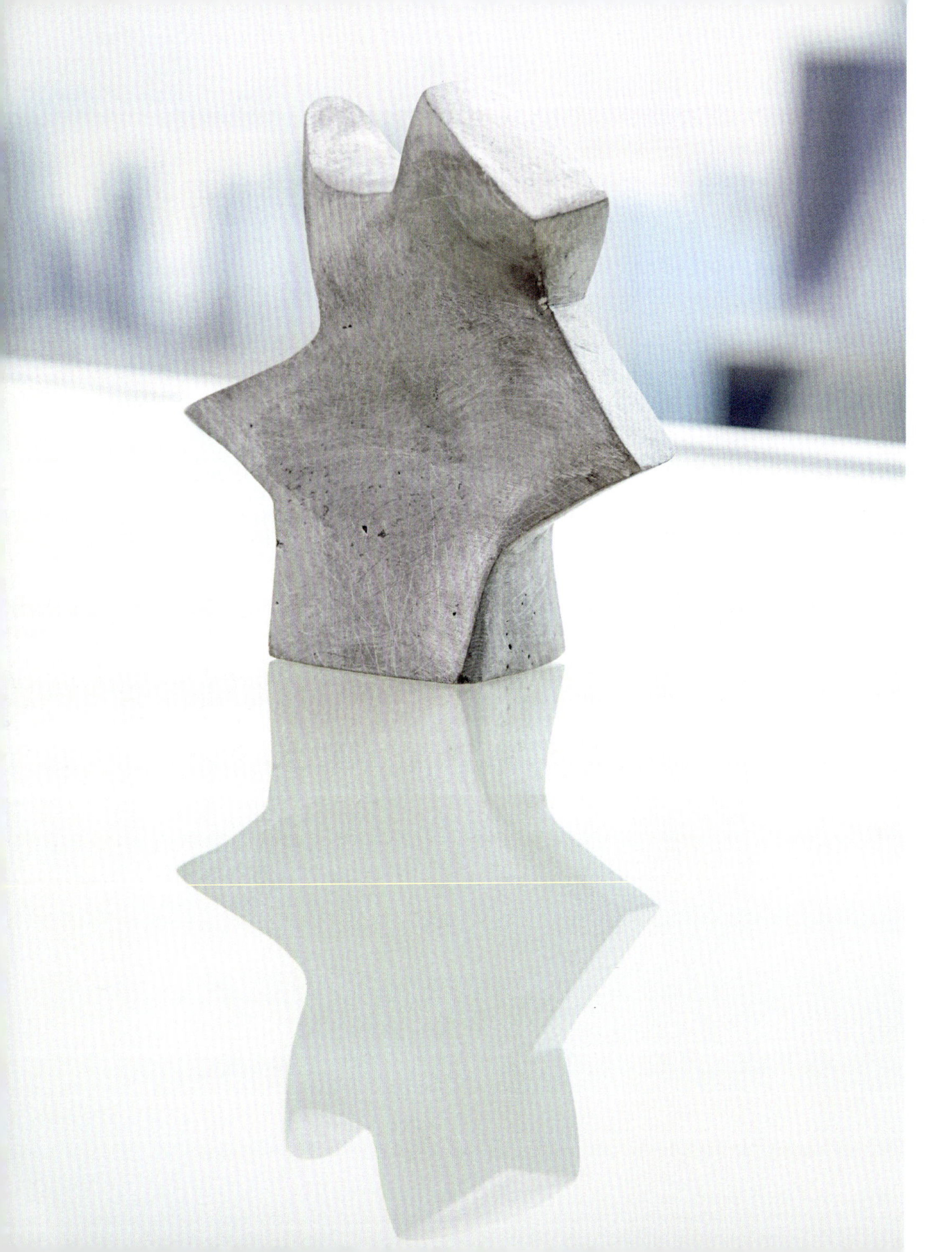

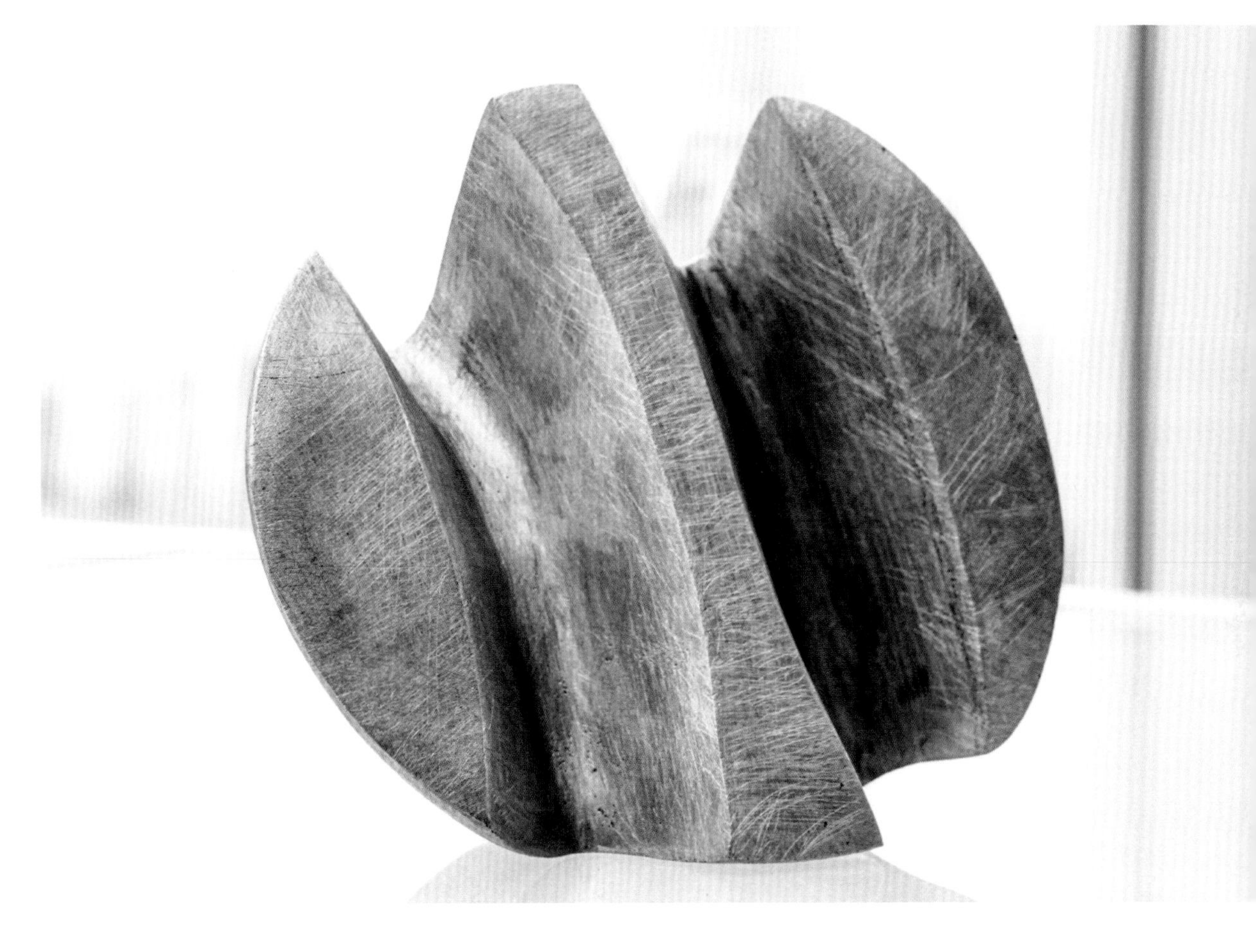

LEFT: **ALEPH**, ALUMINIUM, 15 X 10 X 6 CM, 2012. ABOVE: **SHHH**, ALUMINIUM,12 X 19 X 10 CM, 2013

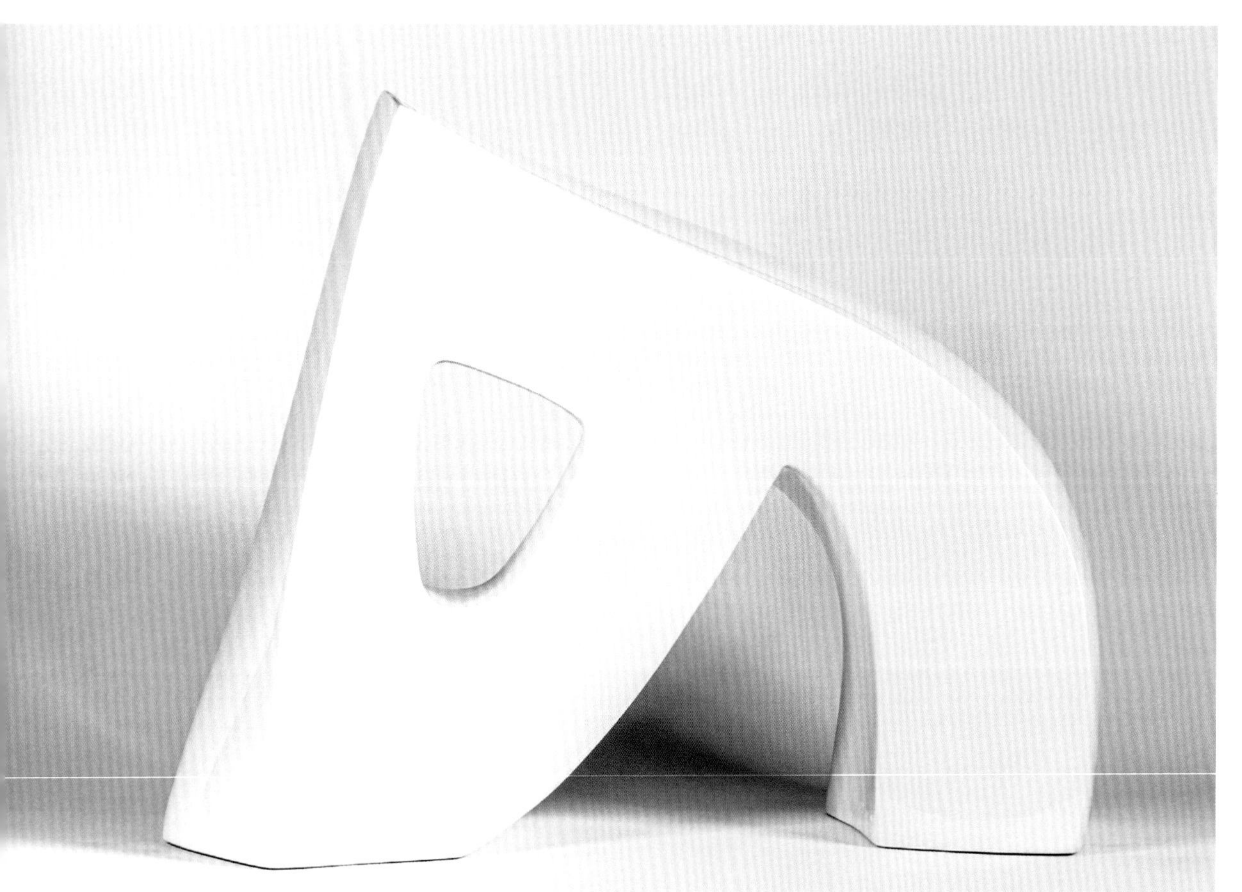

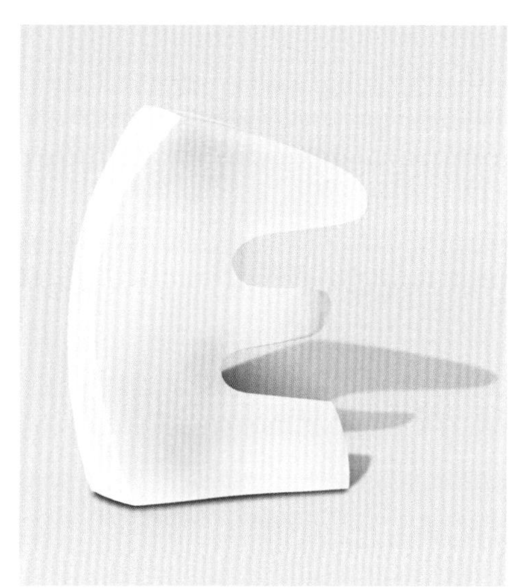

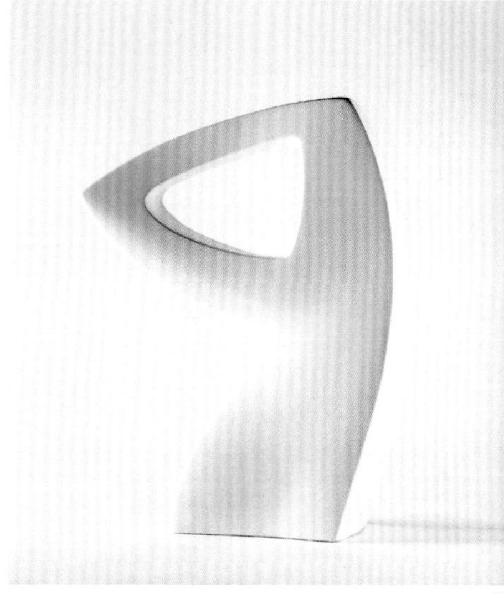

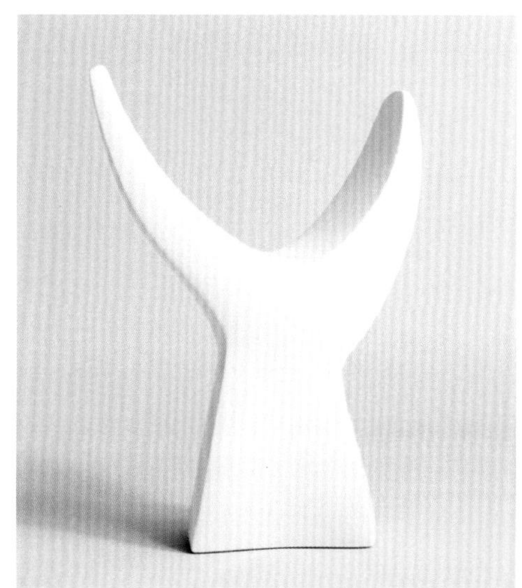

ABOVE: **RESH**, 50 X 37 X 17 CM, 2014
TOP LEFT: **HÉ**, 58 X 55 X 16 CM, 2017
BOTTOM LEFT: **WAW**, 58 X 46 X 16 CM, 2014
OPPOSITE PAGE: **BEIT**, 65 X 81 X 37 CM, 2014

ALL WORKS GLASS FIBRE AND RESIN,
AUTOMOTIVE PAINT

'I EXPERIMENT WITH WORKS AT DIFFERENT SCALES. I AM INTERESTED BY THE INSTABILITY OF SCALE, AND HOW DECEPTIVE IT CAN BE WHEN IT LACKS A FRAME OF REFERENCE. I ALWAYS START WITH A SMALL MODEL AND, WHEN IT IS ENLARGED TO THE DESIRED SIZE, THE RESULT CANNOT ALWAYS BE FORETOLD.

CONTEXT, VANTAGE POINT AND
RELATIONSHIP TO SPACE ARE ALL
ELEMENTS THAT INFLUENCE THE
VISUAL EFFECT AND IMPACT THE
SCALING-UP PROCESS. AS WORKS
BECOME LARGER, THE ARTICULATION
OF SPACE STARTS SUPERSEDING
OTHER CONSIDERATIONS; SPACE
BECOMES ATMOSPHERE AND VOLUME.'

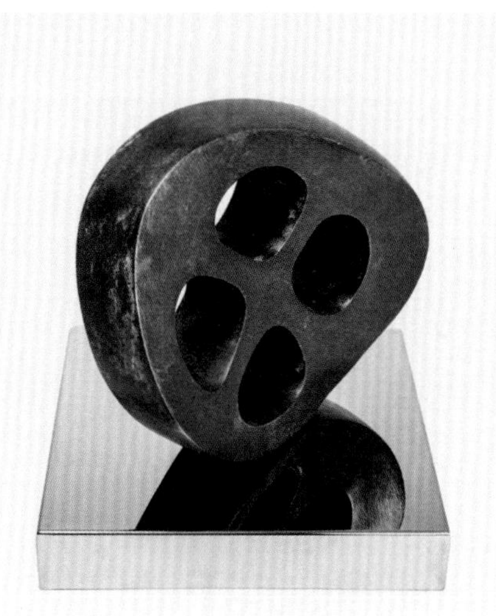

ABOVE: **SHIELD**, 36 X 34 X 34 CM, 2014
RIGHT: **LAMED**, 68 X 60 X 30 CM, 2016
OPPOSITE PAGE: **UNKNOWN**, 65 X 62 X 62 CM, 2012

ALL WORKS BRASS,
MIRRORED STAINLESS STEEL

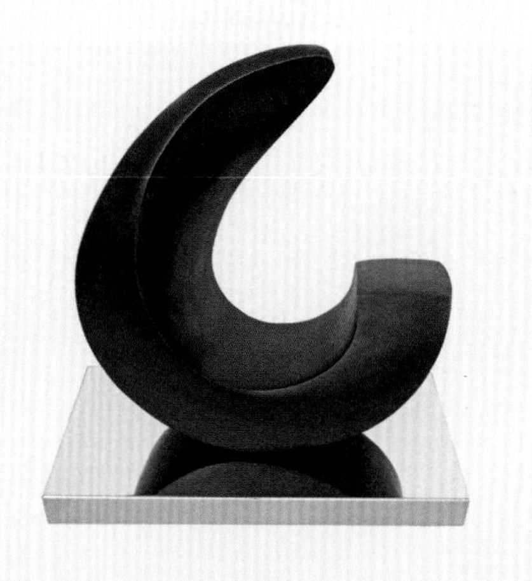

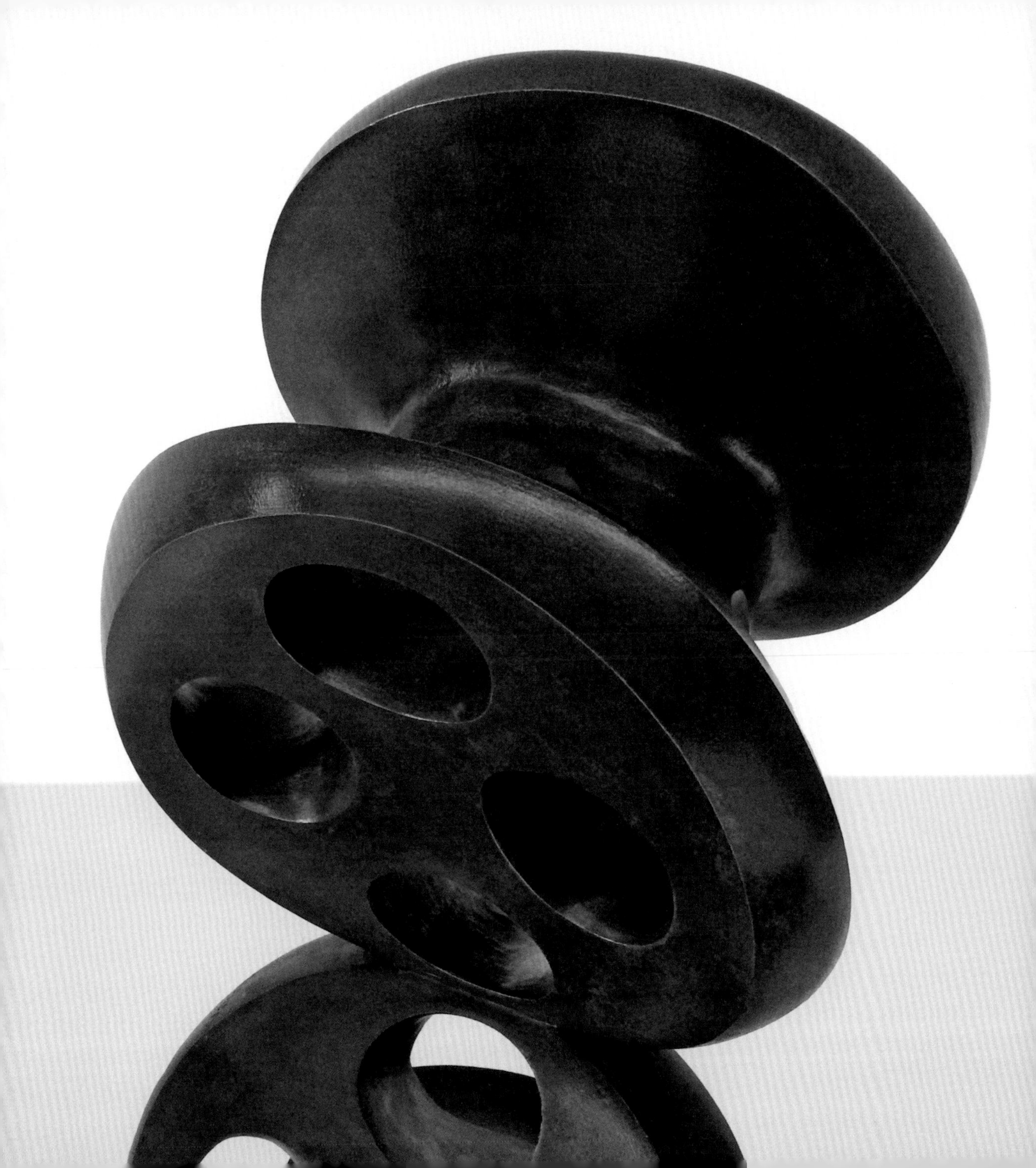

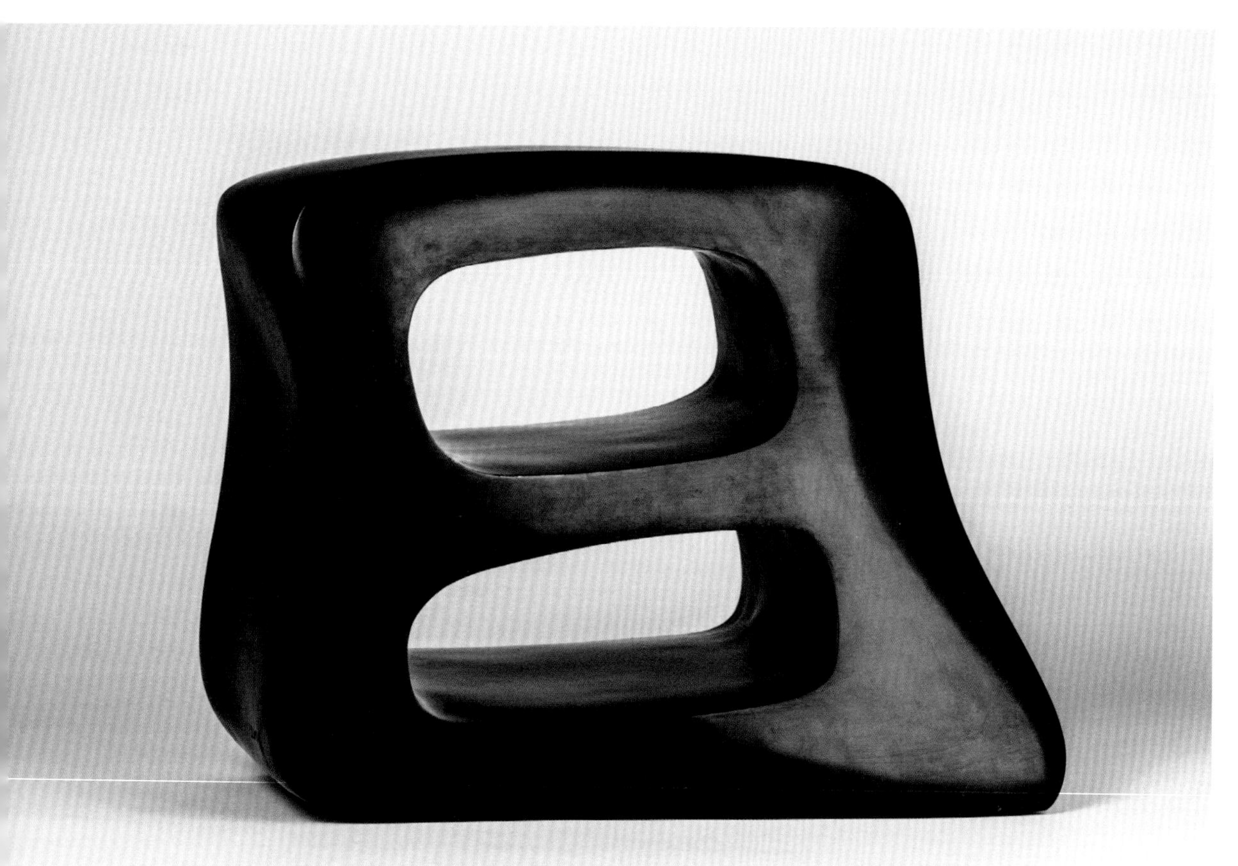

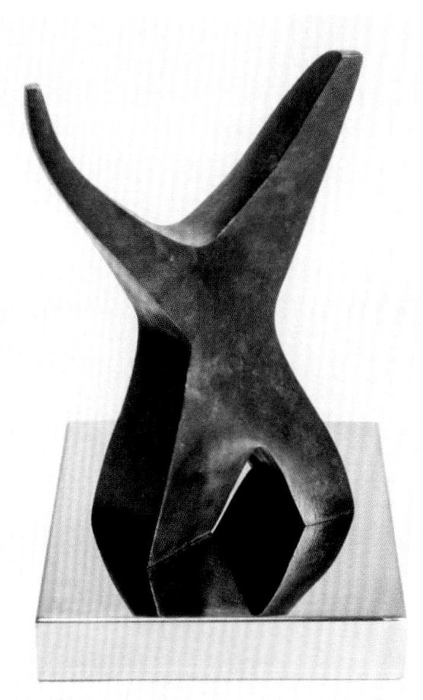

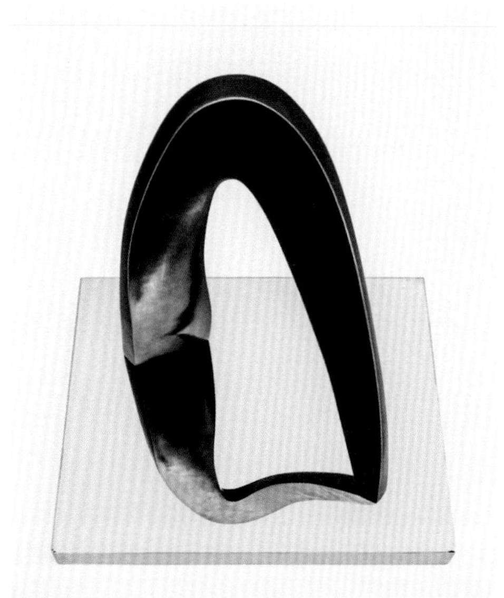

LEFT: **GIMEL**, 49 X 40 X 40 CM, 2014
ABOVE: **TAW**, 46 X 28 X 28 CM, 2014
OPPOSITE PAGE: **HETH**, 35 X 38 X 22 CM, 2014

ALL WORKS BRASS,
MIRRORED STAINLESS STEEL

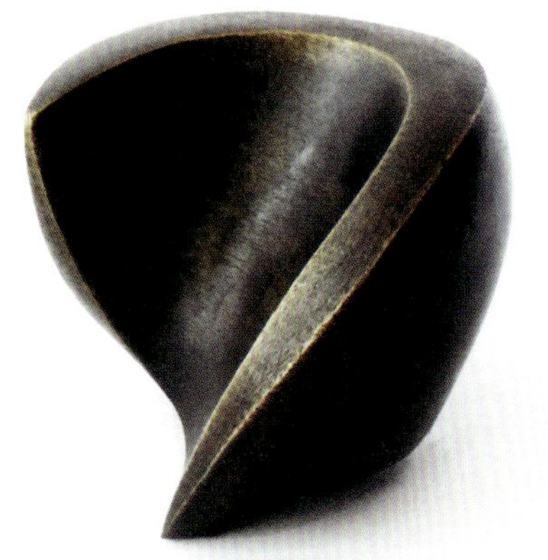

ABOVE: **L3D**, BRONZE, 9 X 10 X 10 CM, 2013. RIGHT: **MEM**, BRASS, 173 X 68 X 38 CM, 2015

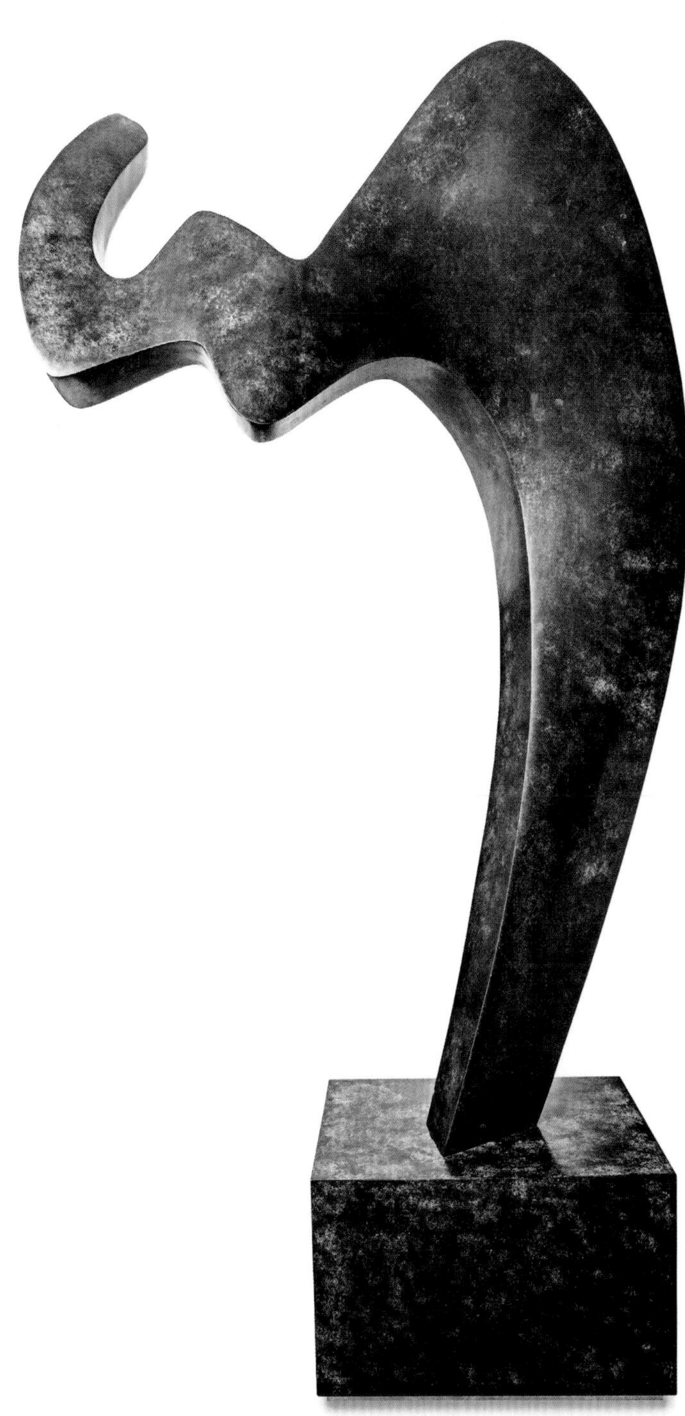

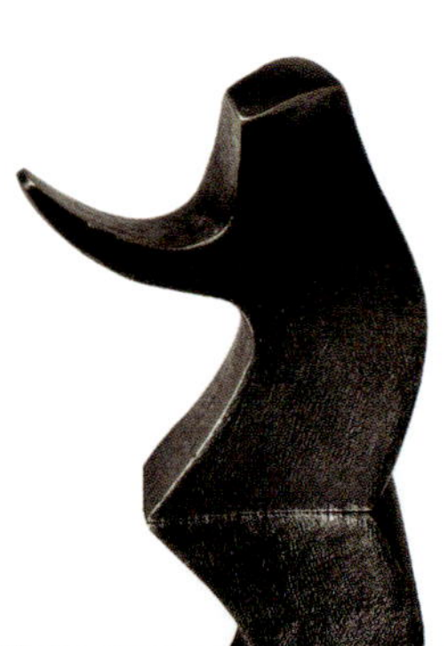

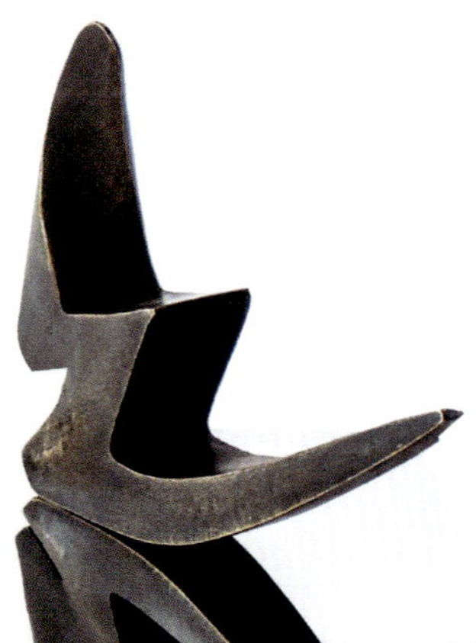

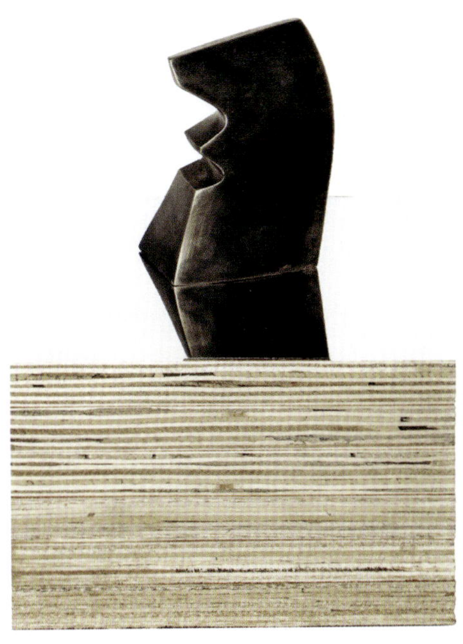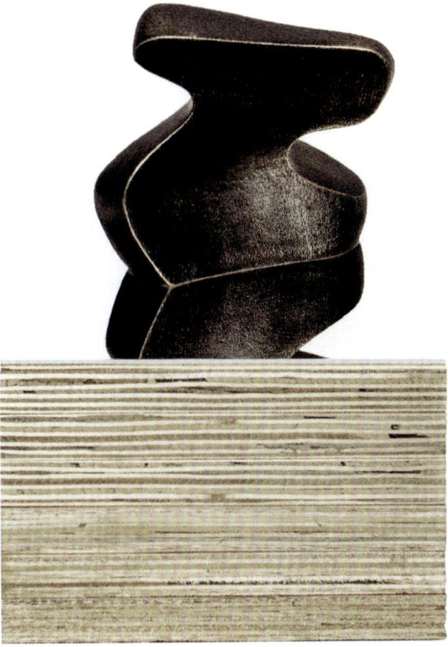

FROM LEFT TO RIGHT:
WAW, 20 X 15 X 15 CM, 2014
SHIN, 21 X 15 X 15 CM, 2014
HÉ, 20 X 15 X 15 CM, 2014
ZAYIN, 26 X 15 X 15 CM, 2017

ALL WORKS BRONZE, PLYWOOD AND
MIRRORED STAINLESS STEEL

SCRABBLE | WORDS

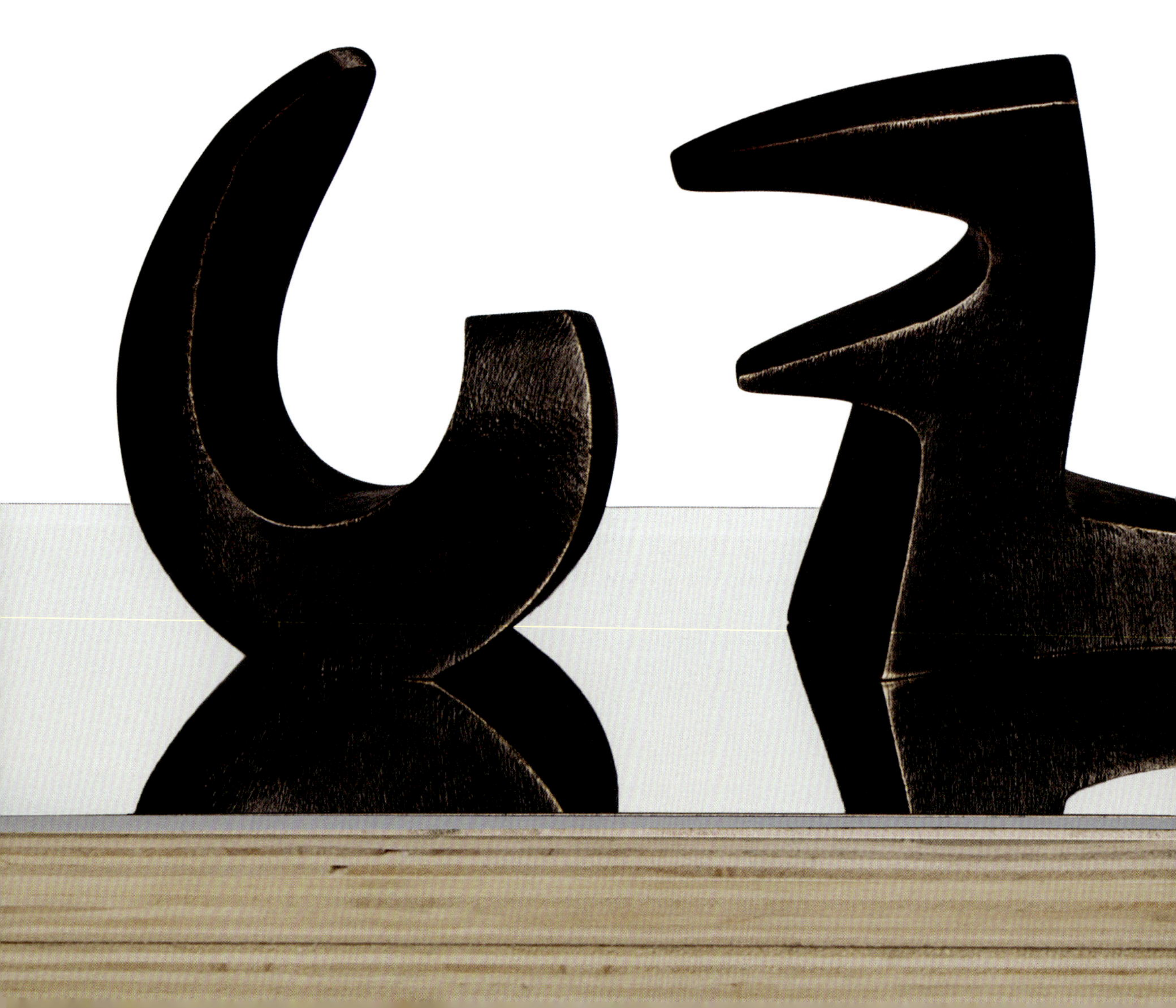

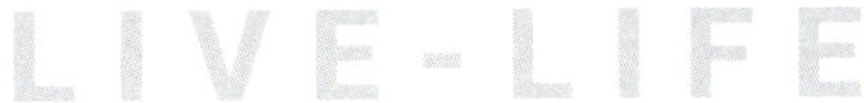

19 X 45 X 15 CM, 2016

ALL WORKS BRONZE, PLYWOOD AND MIRRORED STAINLESS STEEL

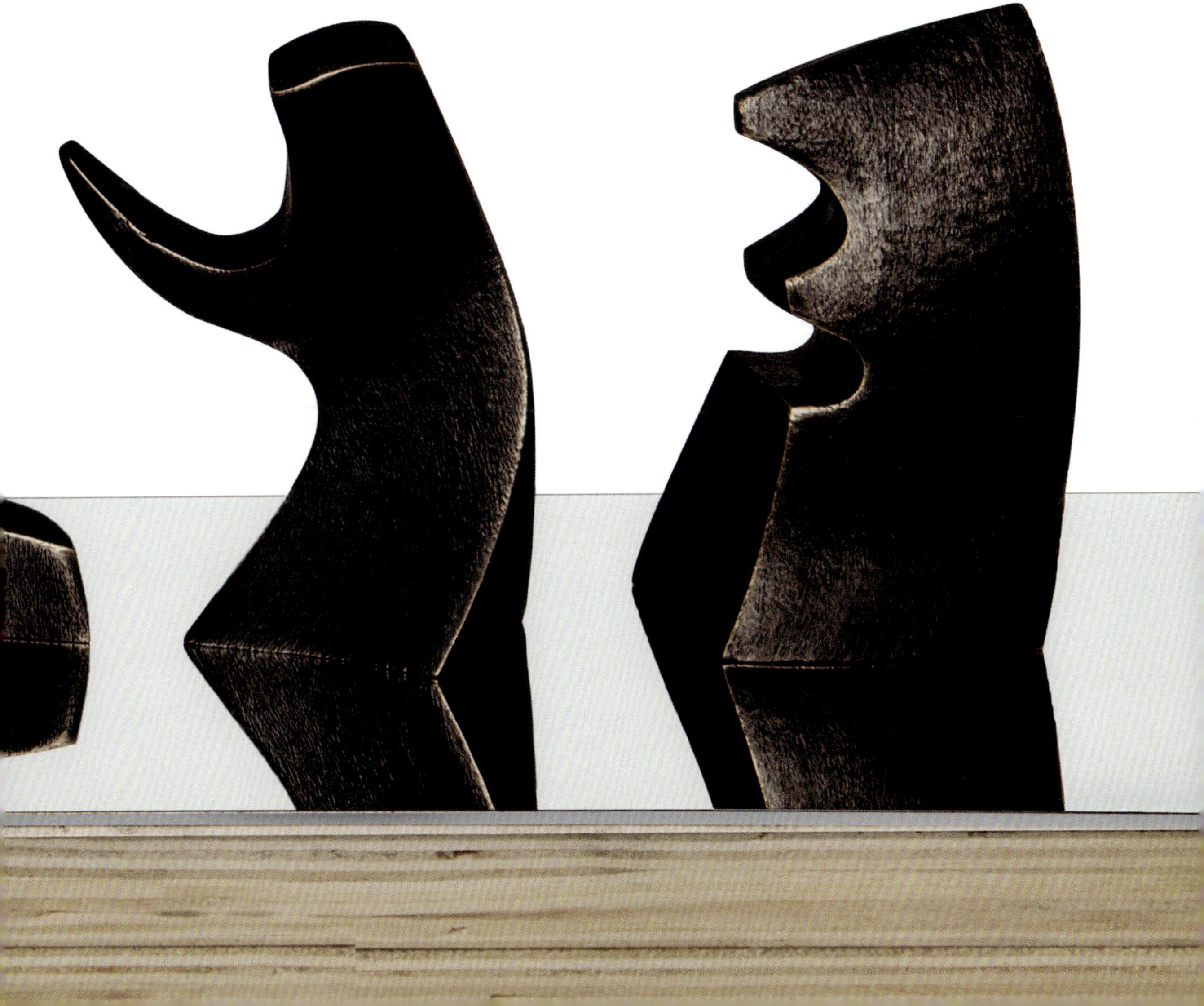

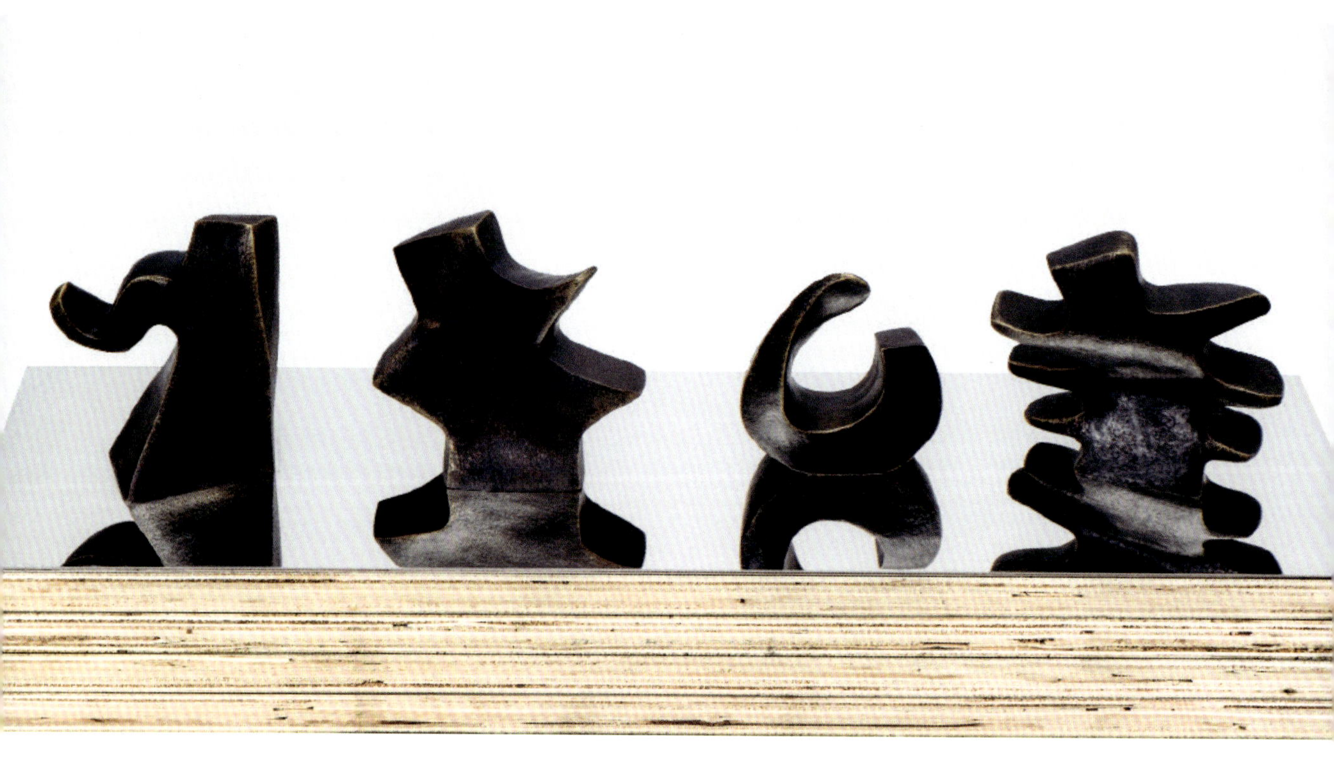

SALAM

21 X 60 X 15 CM, 2014

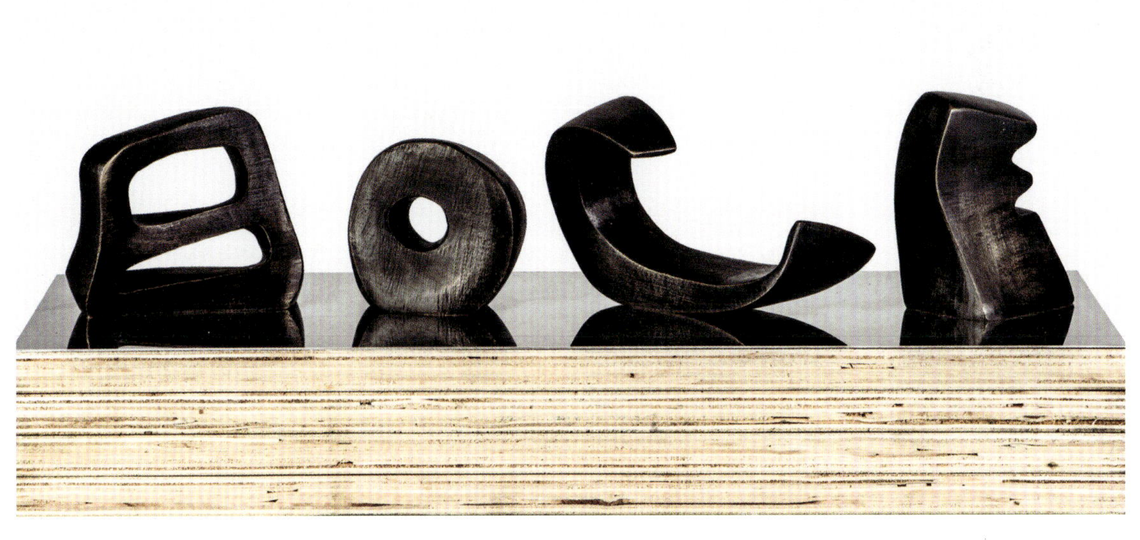

17 X 45 X 15 CM, 2014

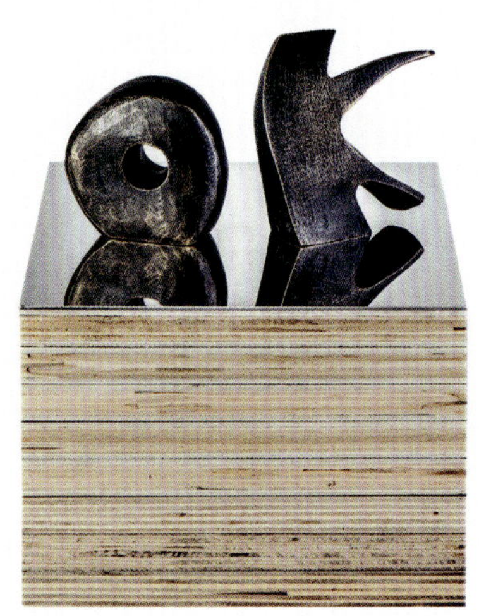

OK-KO

29 X 20 X 20 CM, 2013

HOBB

18 X 30 X 15 CM, 2017

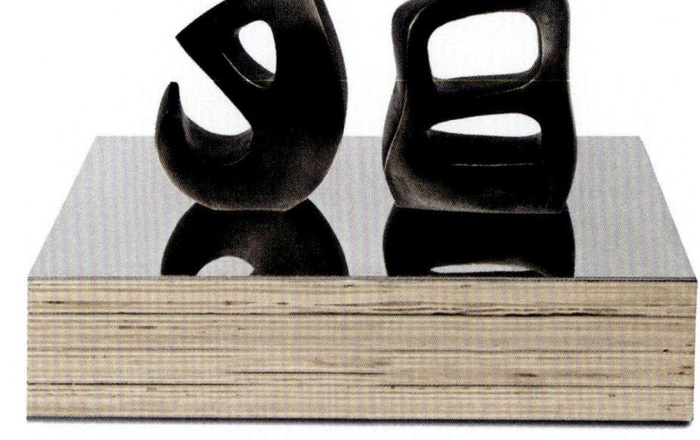

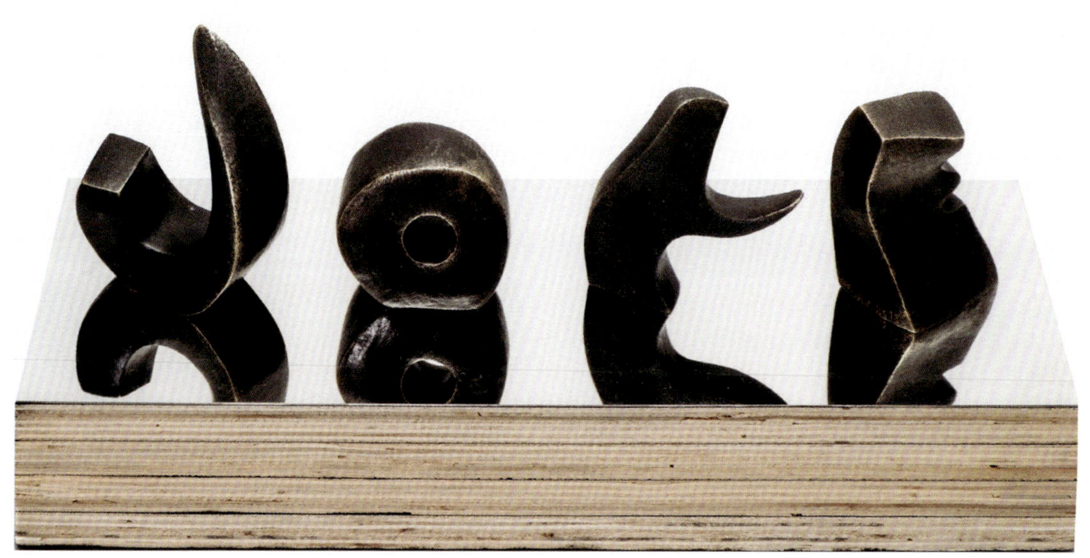

L O V E

18 X 45 X 15 CM, 2013

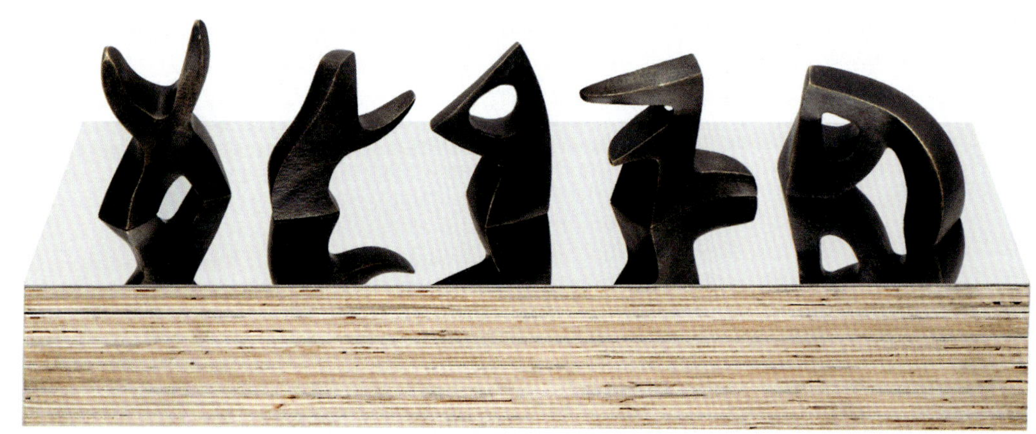

BEIRUT

23 X 60 X 15 CM, 2014

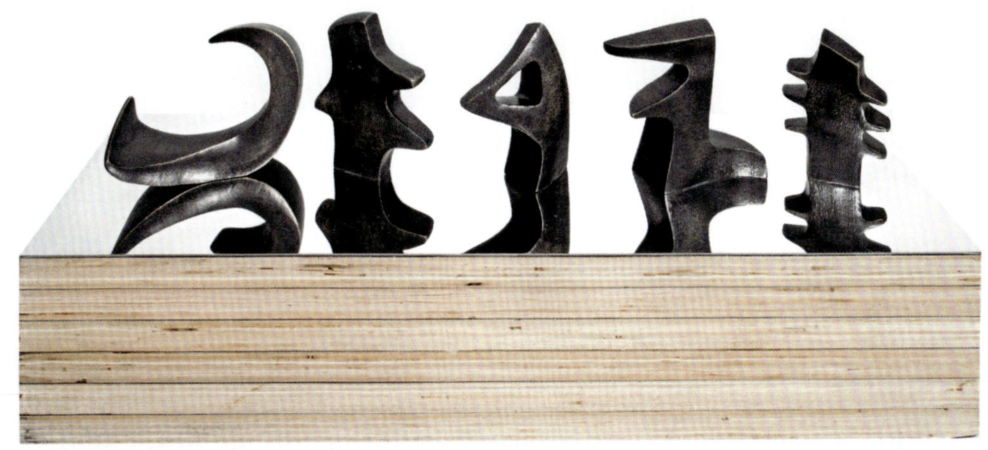

22 X 60 X 15 CM, 2015

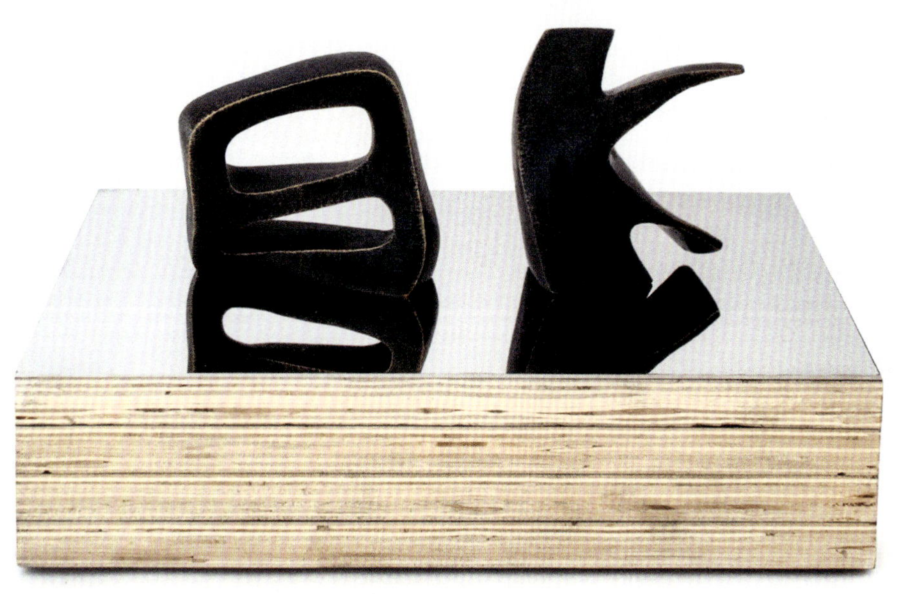

H K

17 X 30 X 15 CM, 2014

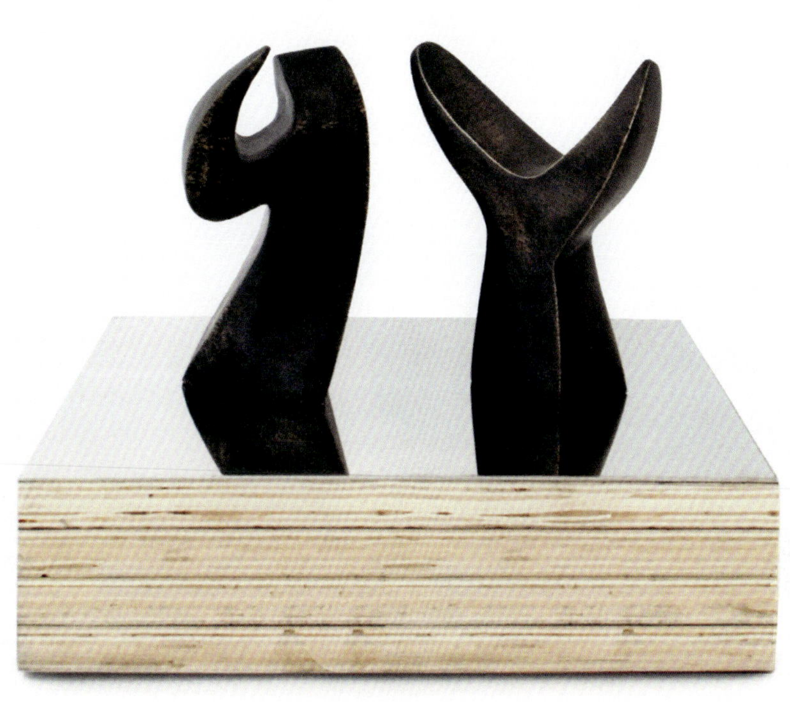

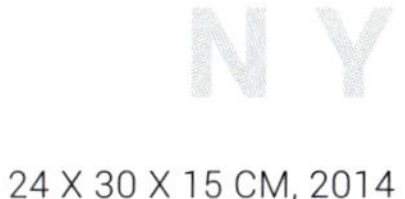

N Y

24 X 30 X 15 CM, 2014

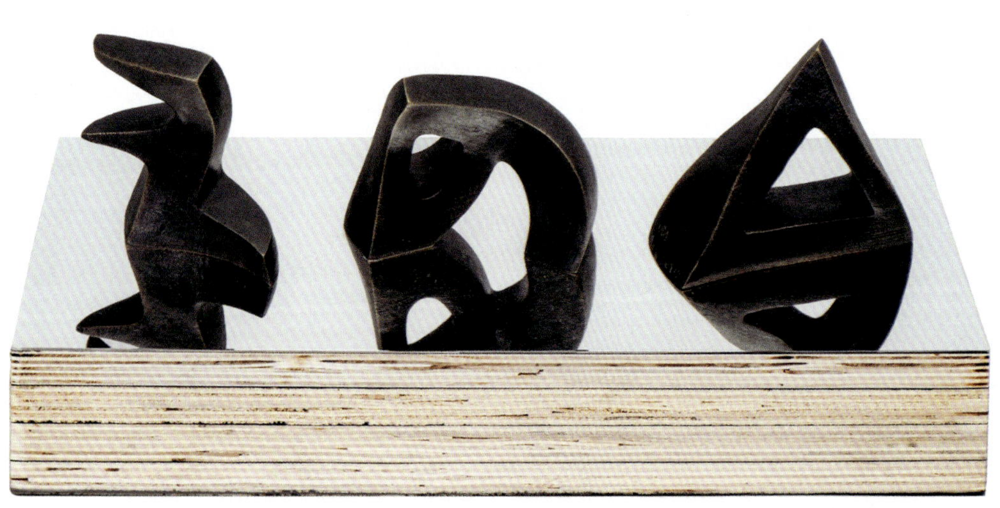

18 X 45 X 15 CM, 2014

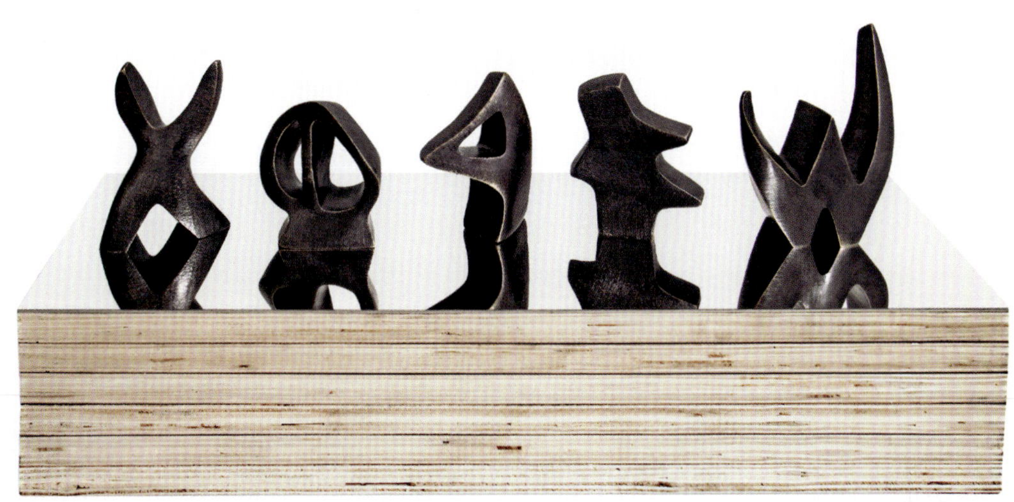

22 X 60 X 15 CM, 2015

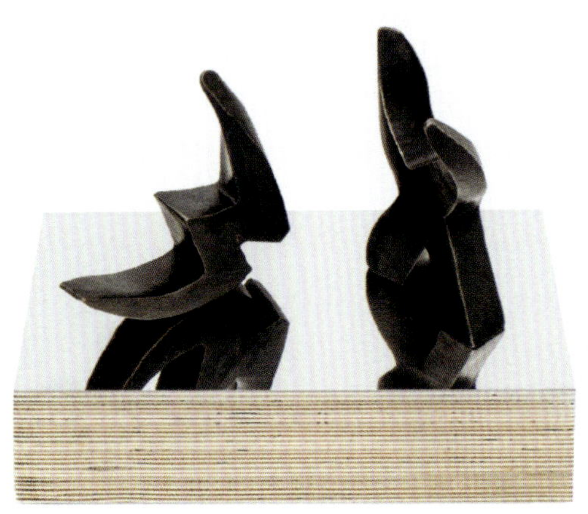

SH.T

22 X 30 X 15 CM, 2014

AH-HA

17 X 30 X 15 CM, 2014

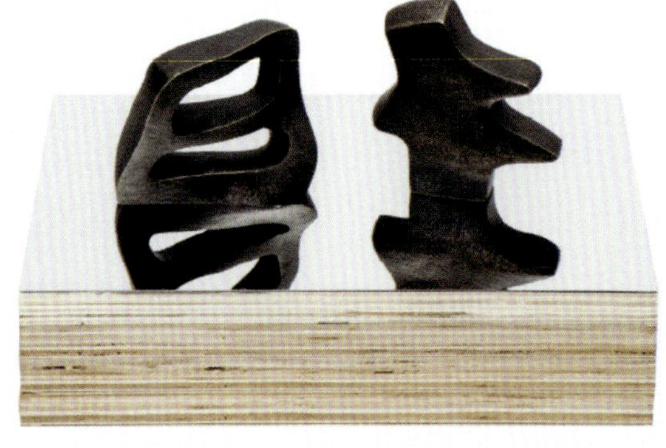

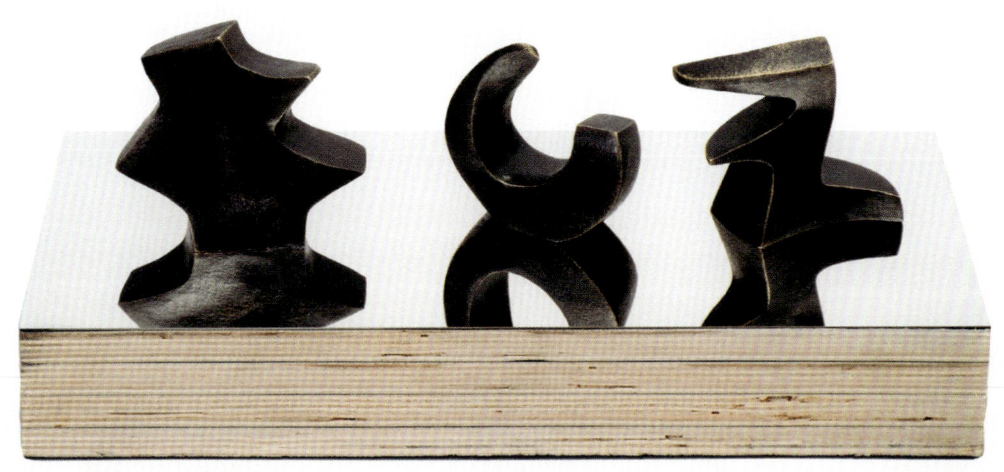

YALLA

18 X 45 X 15 CM, 2014

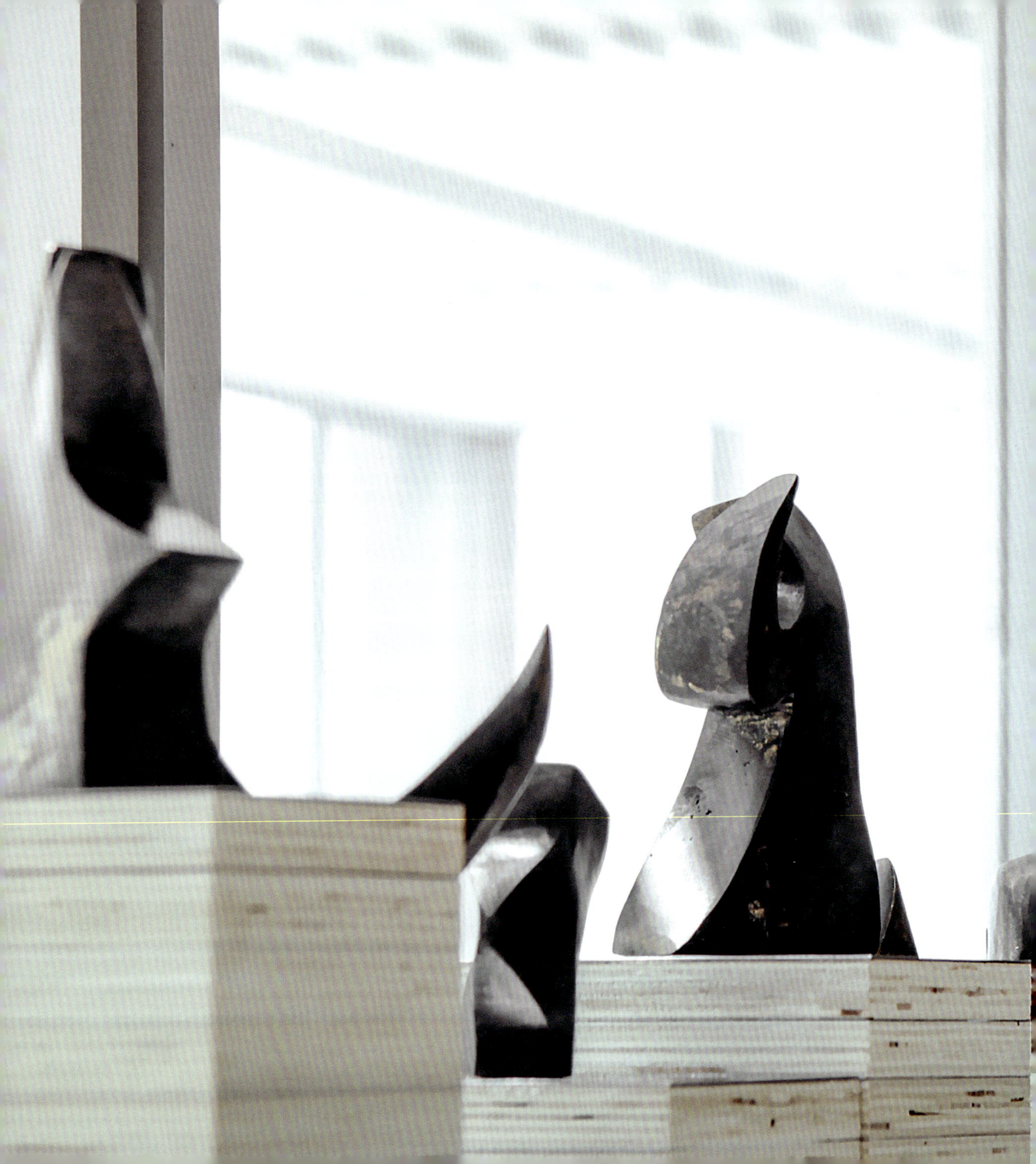

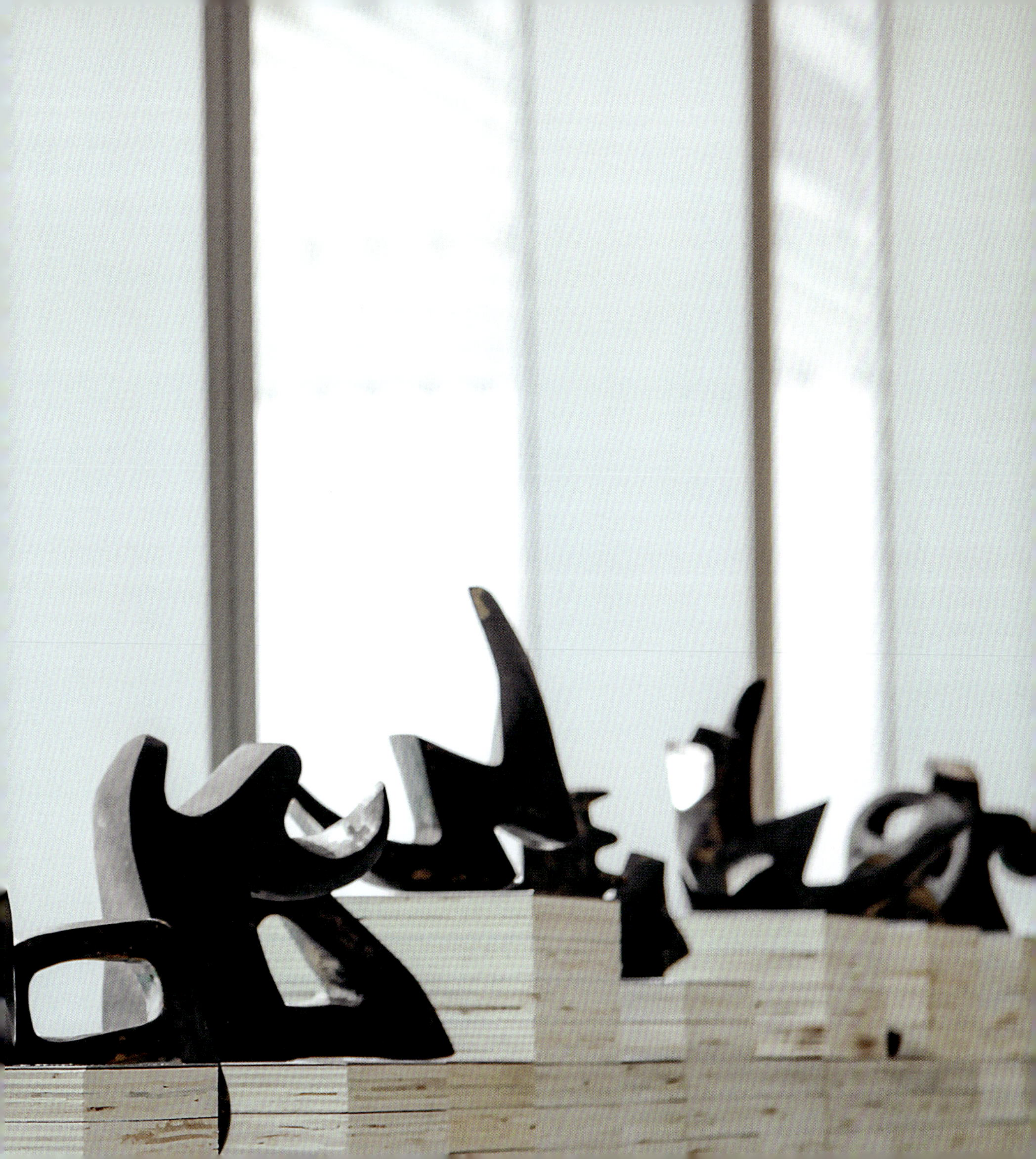

SCRIPTS | MONOGRAMS

'OPTIMISTIC BY NATURE, I BELIEVE
THAT HOPE IS THE VECTOR OF LIFE.
TO ME, ART IS AN ACT THAT IS
IMPLICITLY HOPEFUL: CREATING
SOMETHING THAT HELPS US BREAK
THE SHACKLES, SHIFT THINGS AROUND
SOMEHOW, AND LEAVE TRACES.'

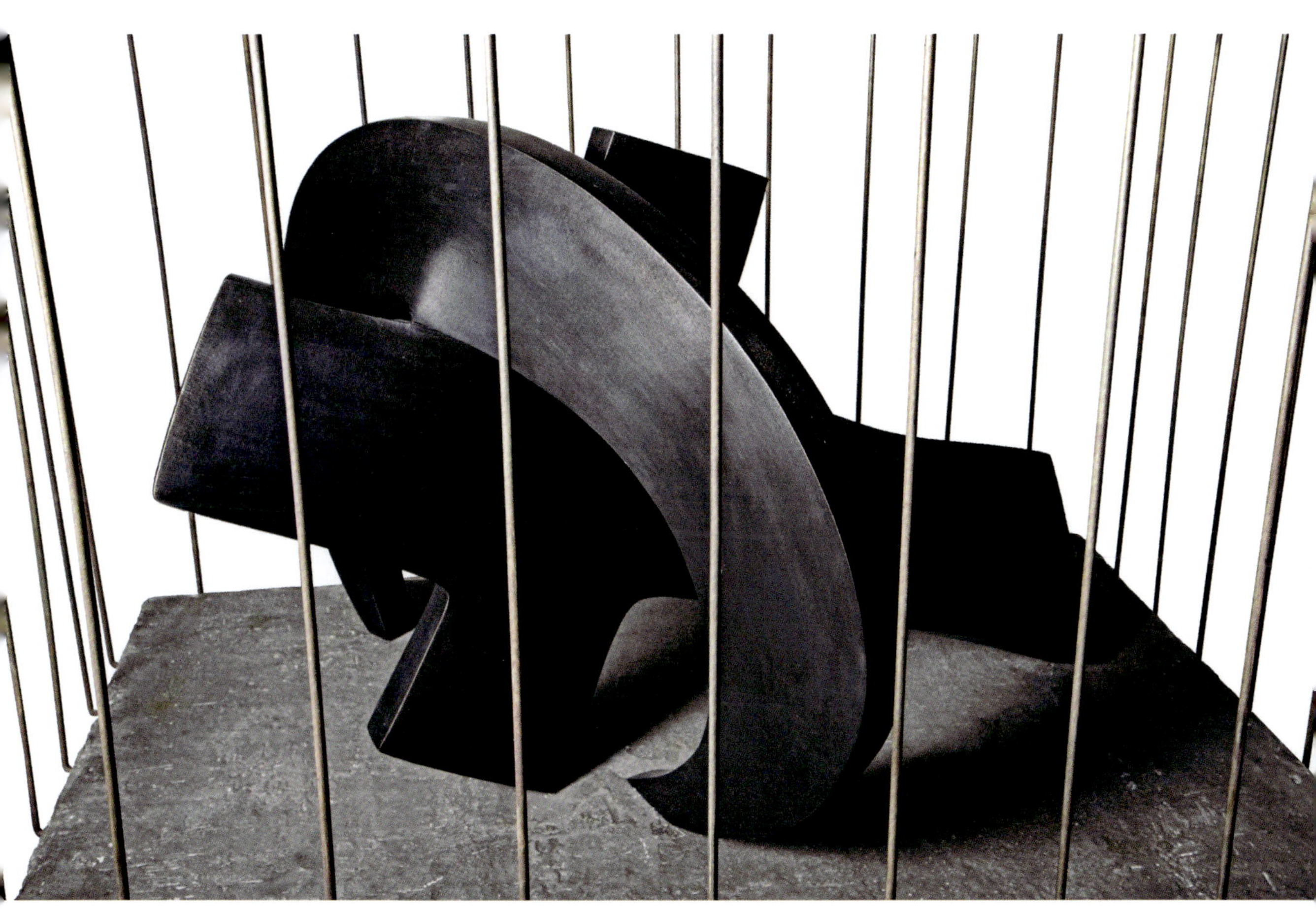

TRAP, BRASS, RESIN, IRON RODS, 167 X 90 X 70 CM, 2016

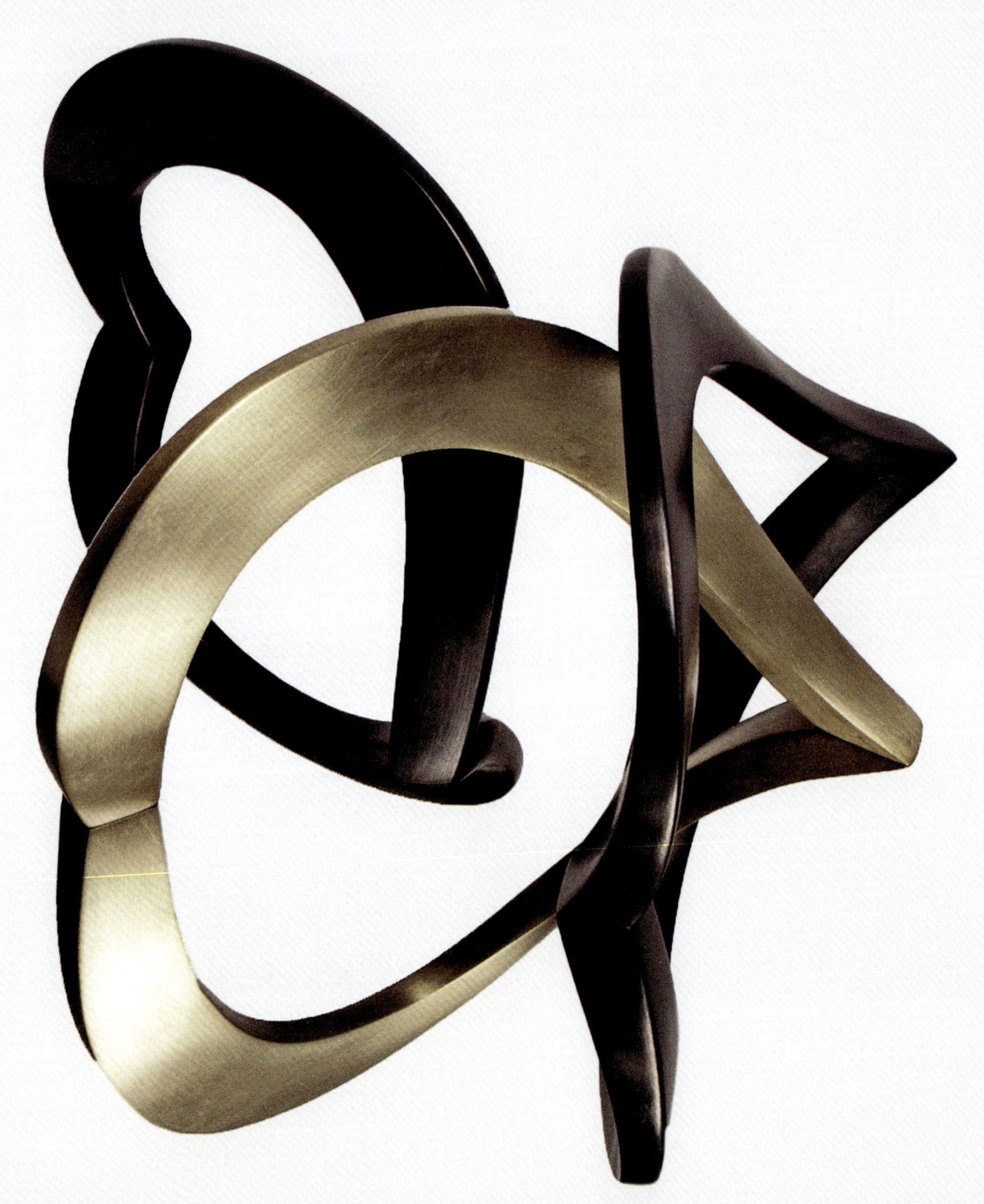

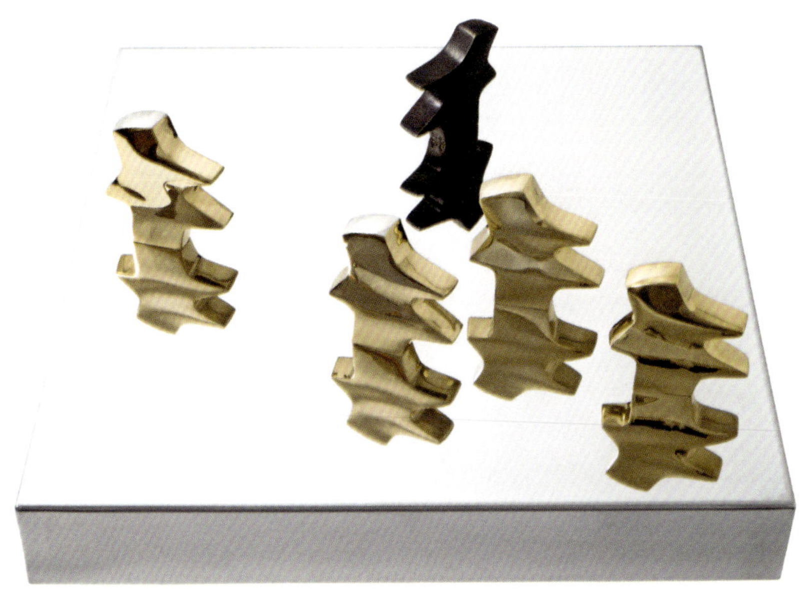

ABOVE: **THE BLACK SHEEP**, BRONZE, GOLD-PLATED BRASS, MIRRORED STAINLESS STEEL, 14 X 58 X 58 CM, 2015
LEFT: **LOVE IS EVERYWHERE III**, BRONZE, MIRRORED STAINLESS STEEL, 15 X 28 X 28 CM, 2017

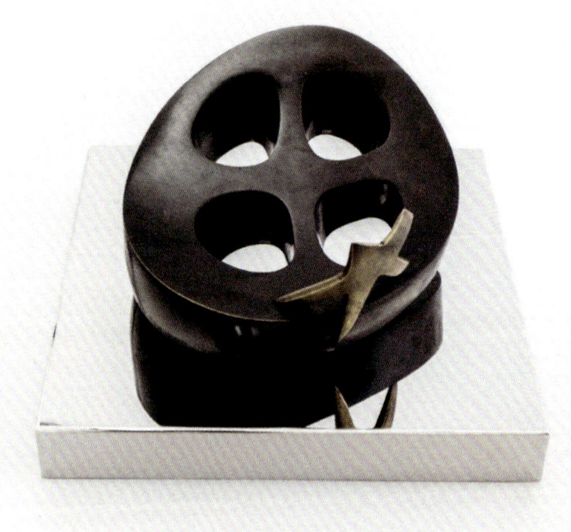

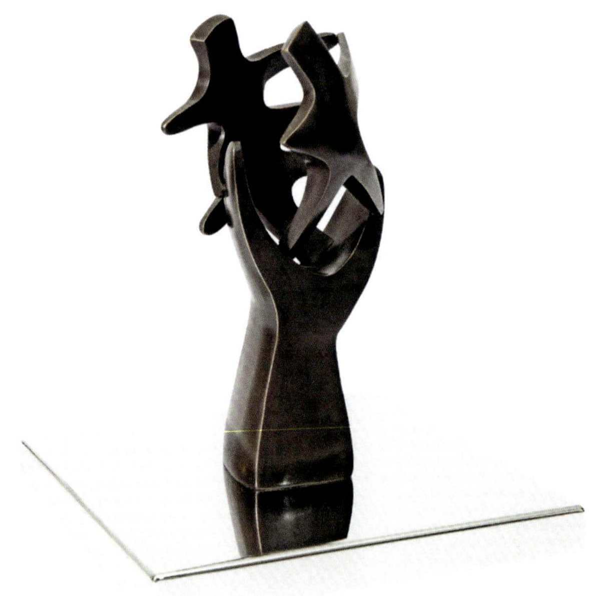

LEFT: **INTO THE UNKNOWN**, BRASS, MIRRORED STAINLESS STEEL, 28 X 44 X 44 CM, 2014
RIGHT: **A TRIOLOGY OF LOVE**, BRONZE, MIRRORED STAINLESS STEEL, 30 X 25 X 25 CM, 2019
OPPOSITE PAGE: **TANGO**, BRONZE, PLYWOOD AND STAINLESS STEEL, 20 X 20 X 20 CM, 2013

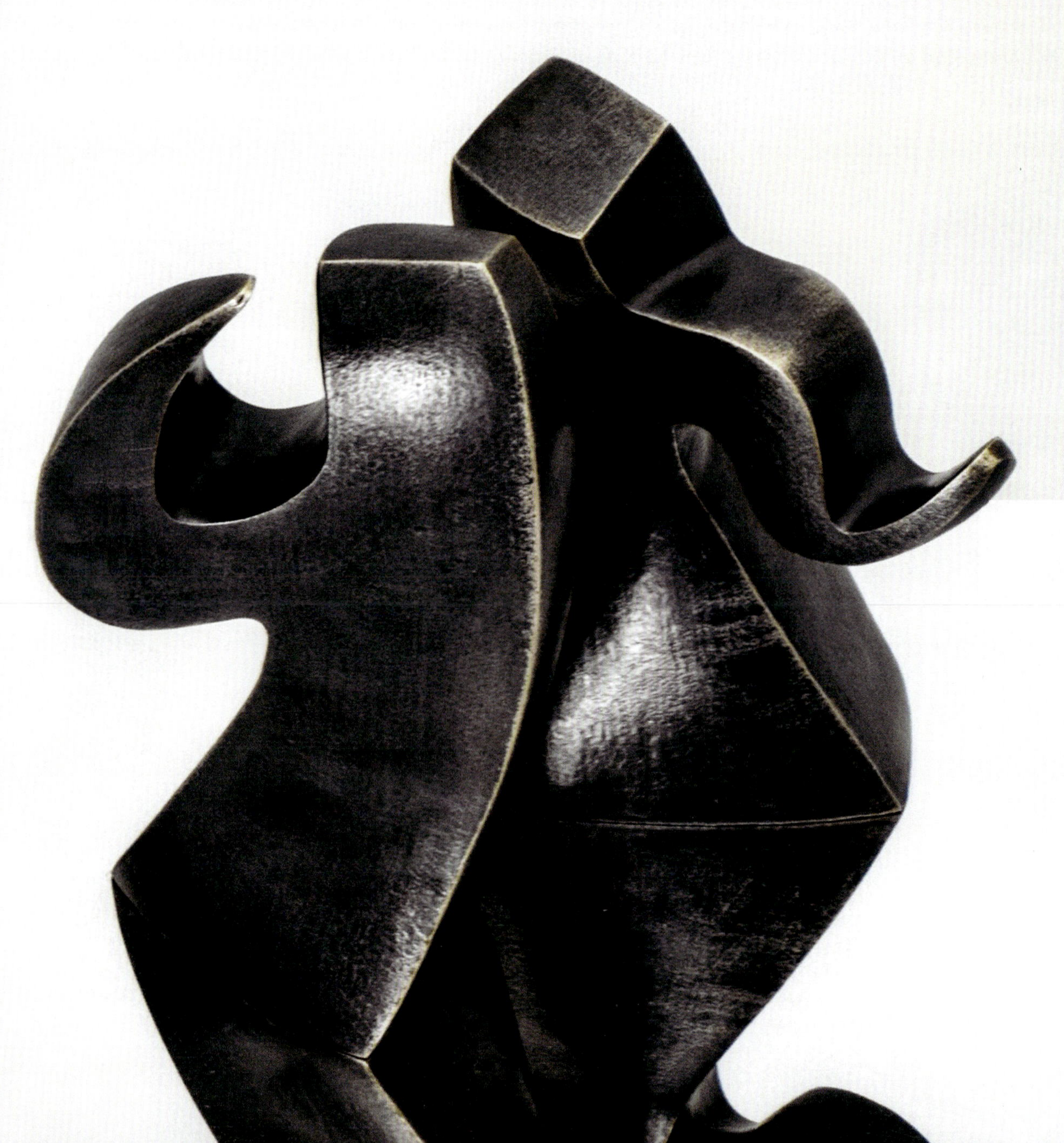

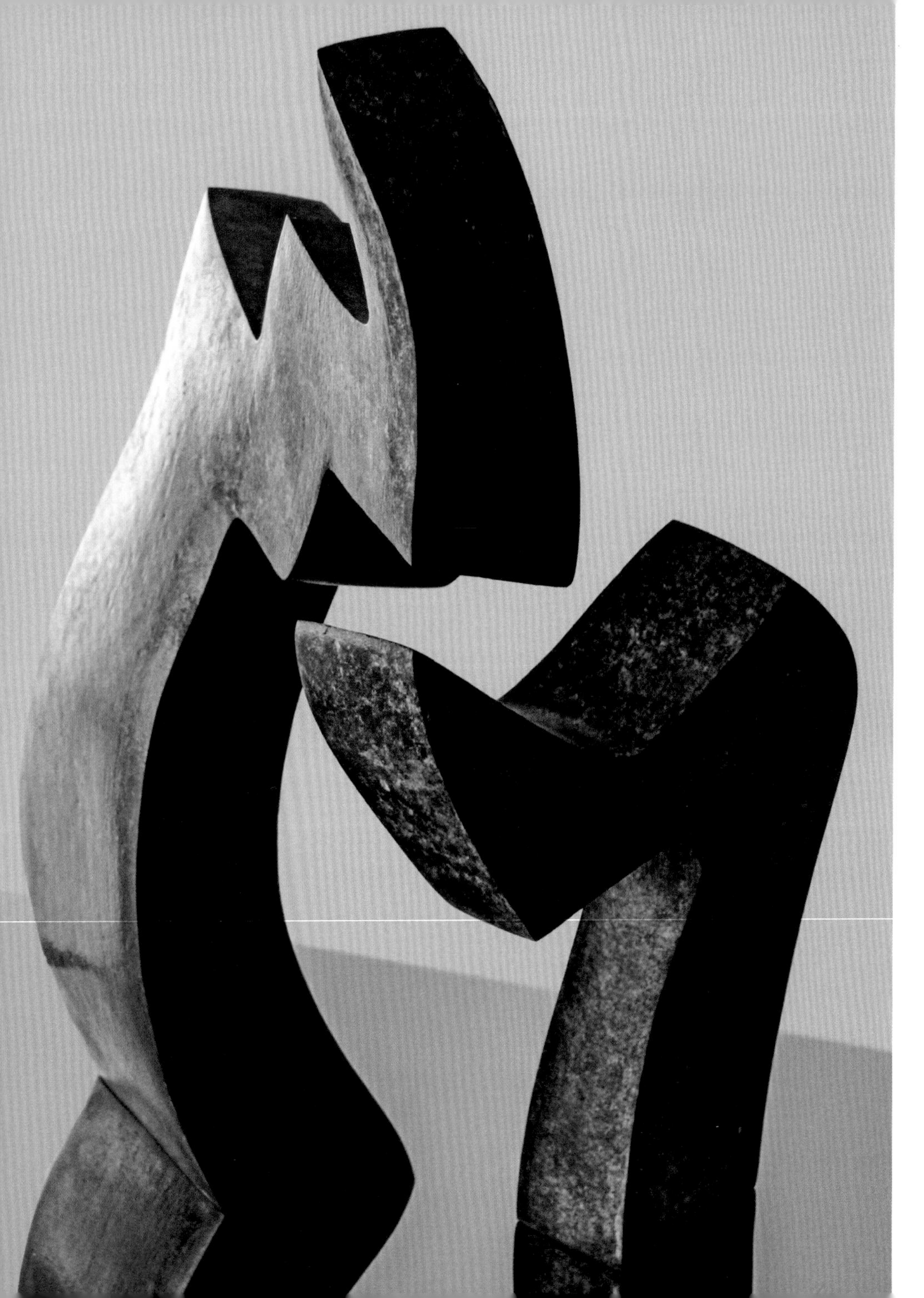

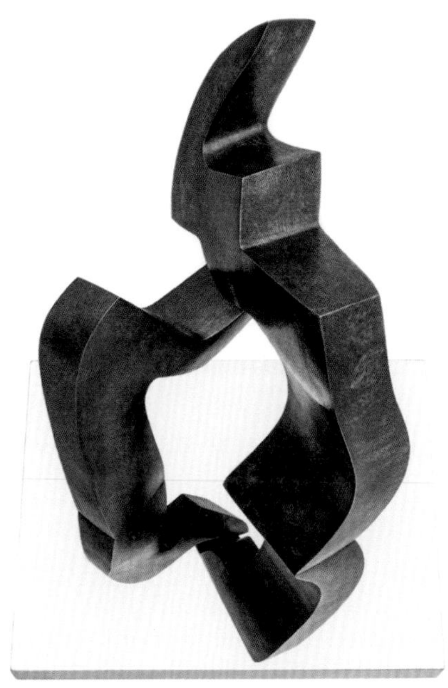

ABOVE AND LEFT: **COMME UN POISSON DANS L'EAU** , BRASS, MIRRORED STAINLESS STEEL, 58 X 58 X 58 CM, 2012
NEXT PAGE: **SALAM**, STEEL, MIRRORED STAINLESS STEEL, 192 X 110 X 110 CM, 2016

'THE YEARLY RENDEZVOUS OF BEIRUT
ART WEEK GAVE ME THE INCENTIVE TO
WORK ON LARGE-SCALE SCULPTURES,
AND THE REWARD TO SEE THEY
THRIVE IN THE CONTEXT OF THE CITY,
INTERACTING WITH PEOPLE IN THEIR
DAILY LIVES. AND TO ME, THE BEAUTY
OF IT WAS THAT IT REACHED PEOPLE OF
ALL WALKS OF LIFE—SOMETIMES WITH
LITTLE OR NO EXPOSURE TO ART, GIVEN
THE LACK OF PUBLIC ART AND ART
MUSEUMS IN LEBANON.'

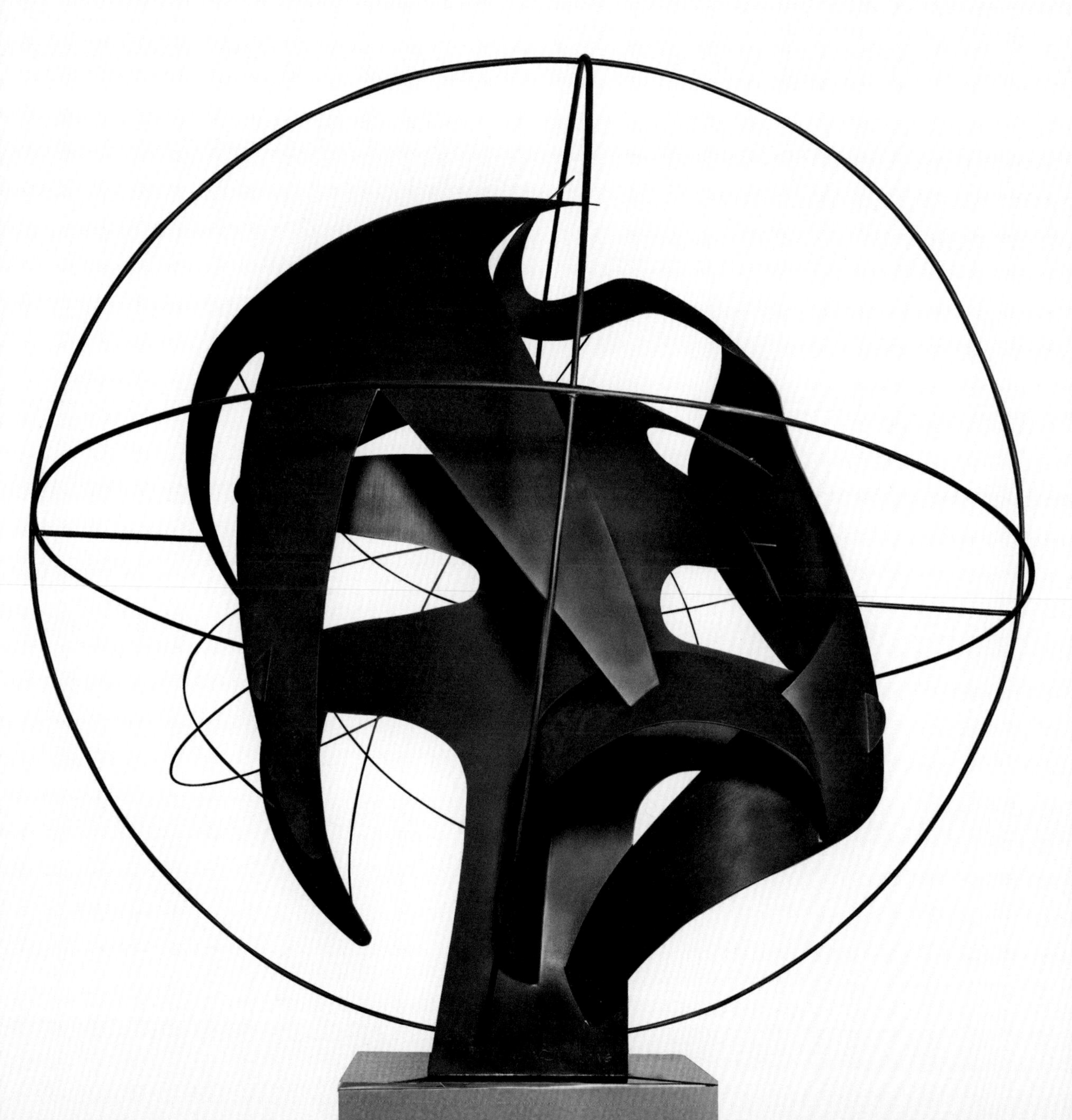

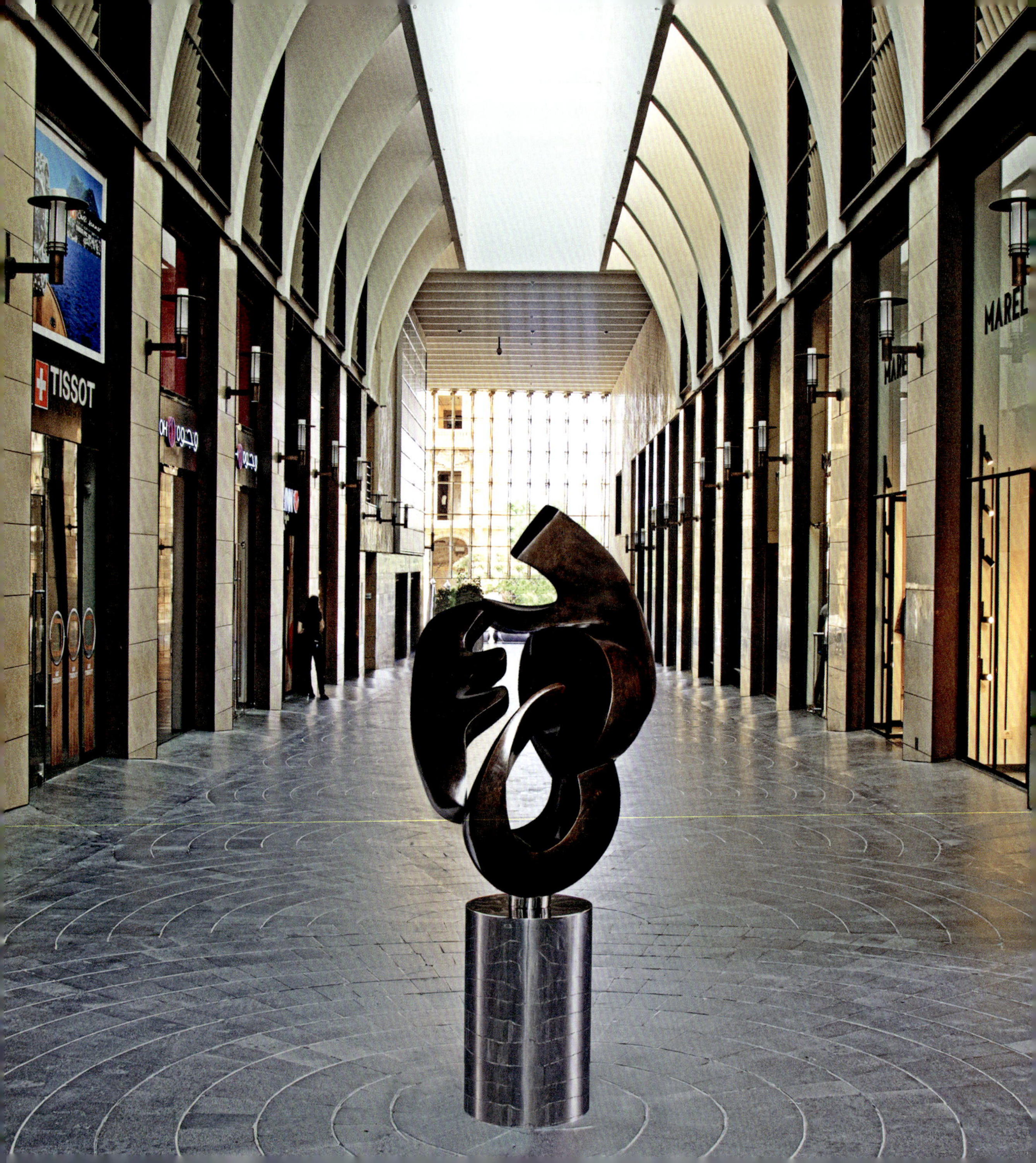

TISSOT
MAREL

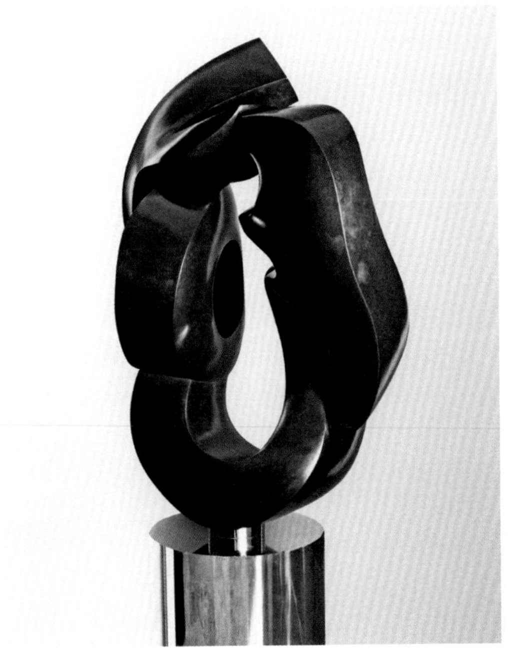

ENTANGLED LOVE, BRASS, MIRRORED STAINLESS STEEL, 185 X 73 X 68 CM, 2015

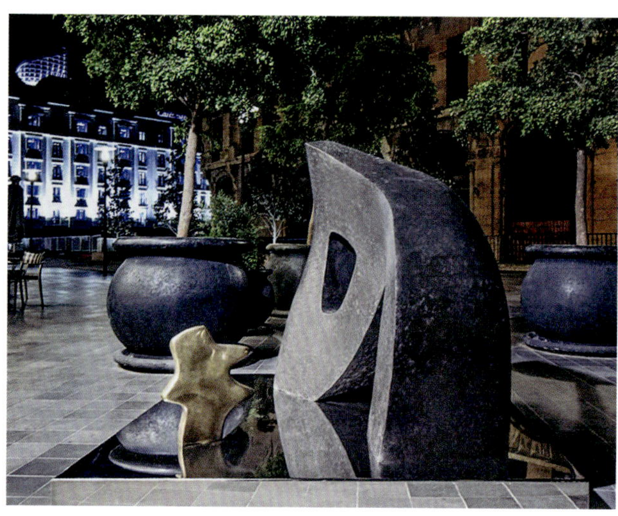

ABOVE: **ALPHABEIT**, BRASS, MIRRORED STAINLESS STEEL, 150 X 180 X 180 CM, 2013
RIGHT: RESIN, BRASS, MIRRORED STAINLESS STEEL, 58 X 72 X 72 CM, 2013

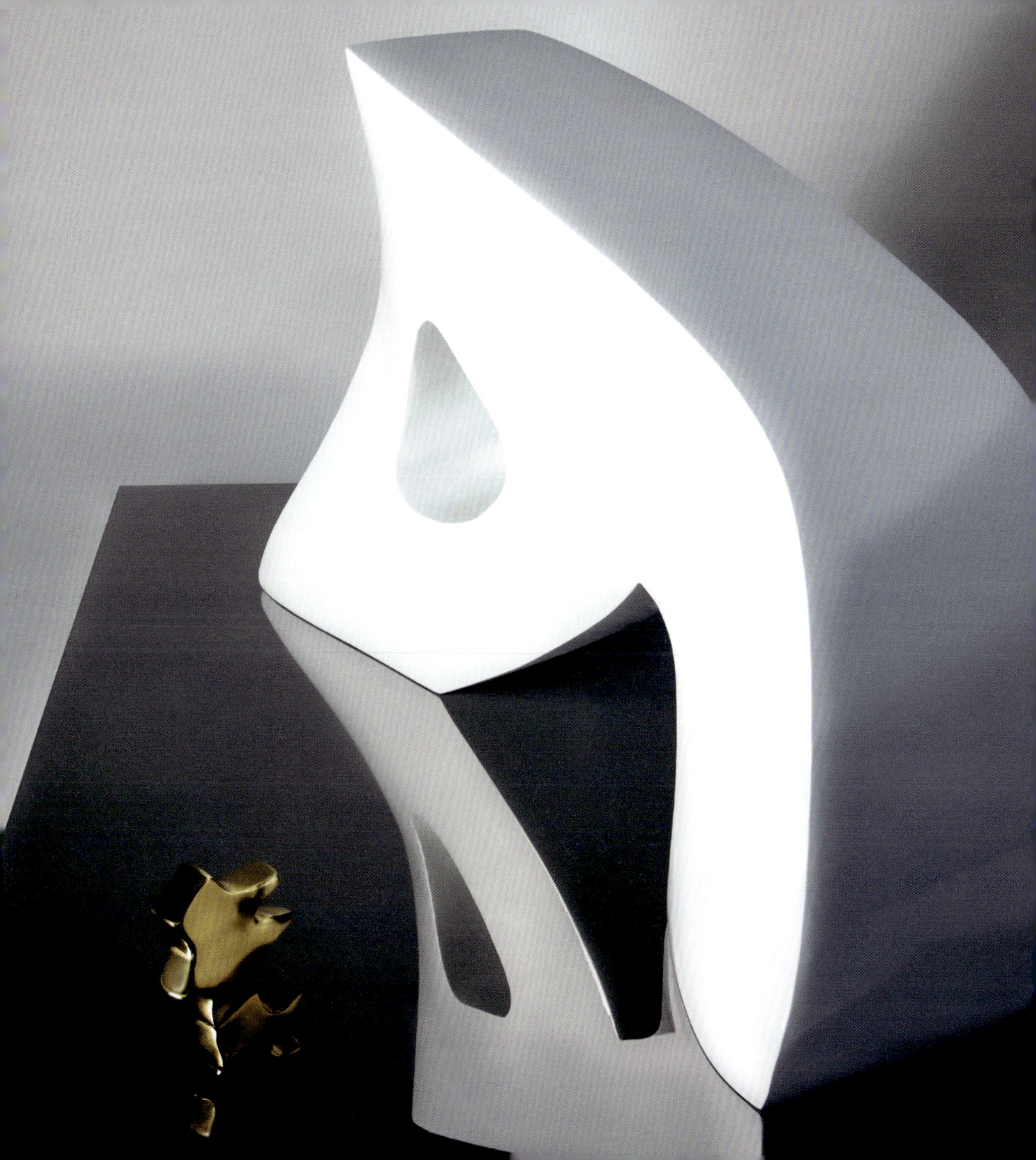

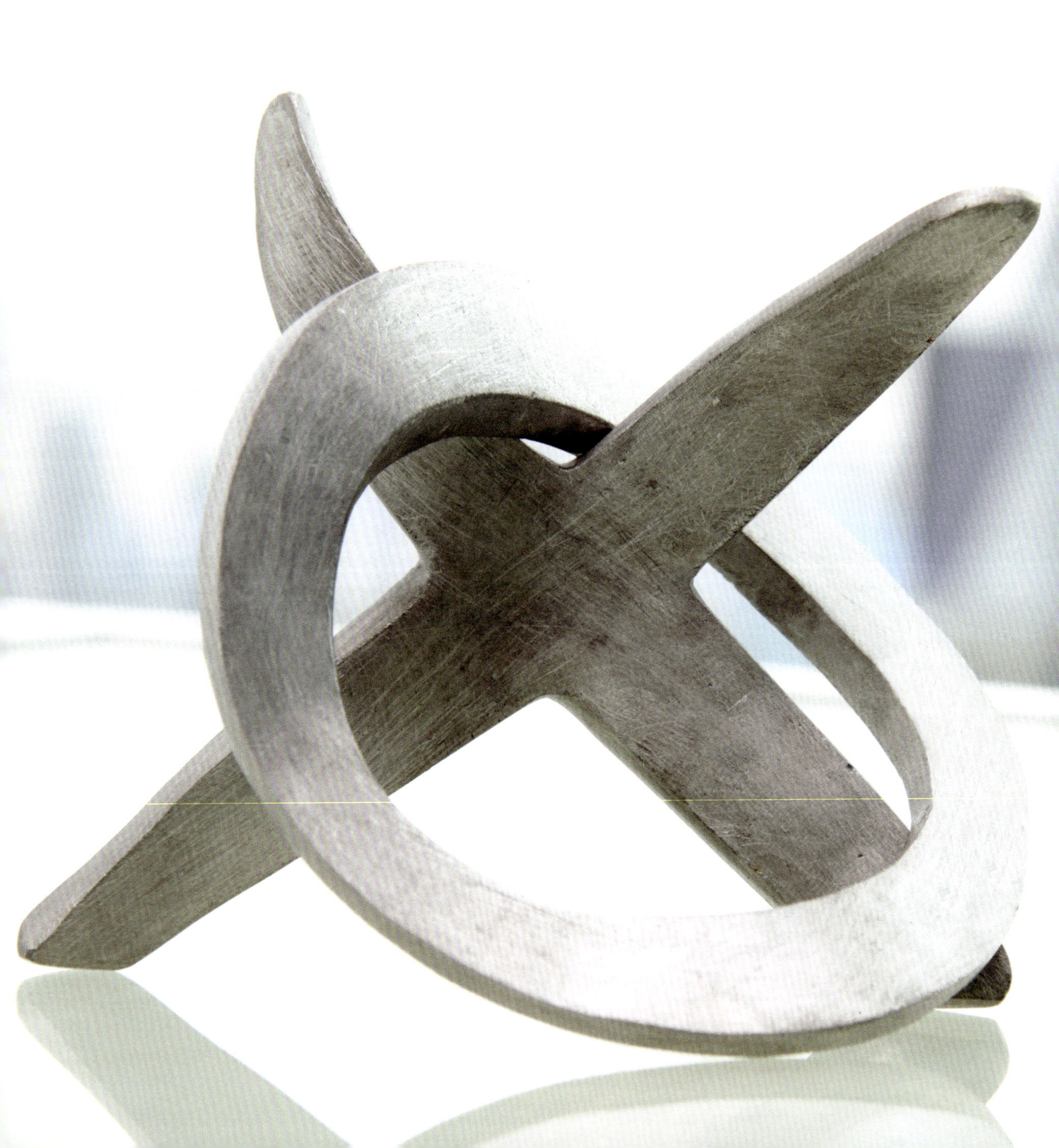

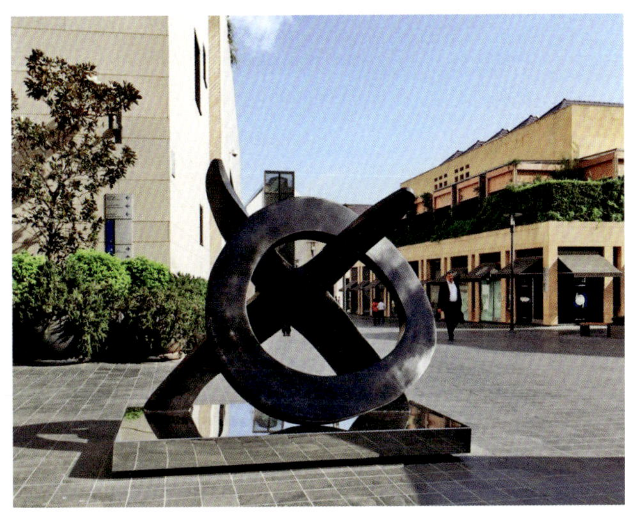

ABOVE: **NOUGHTS AND CROSSES**, PAINTED ALUMINIUM, MIRRORED STAINLESS STEEL, 173 X 190 X 95 CM, 2014
LEFT: ALUMINIUM, 17 X 15 X 18 CM, 2012

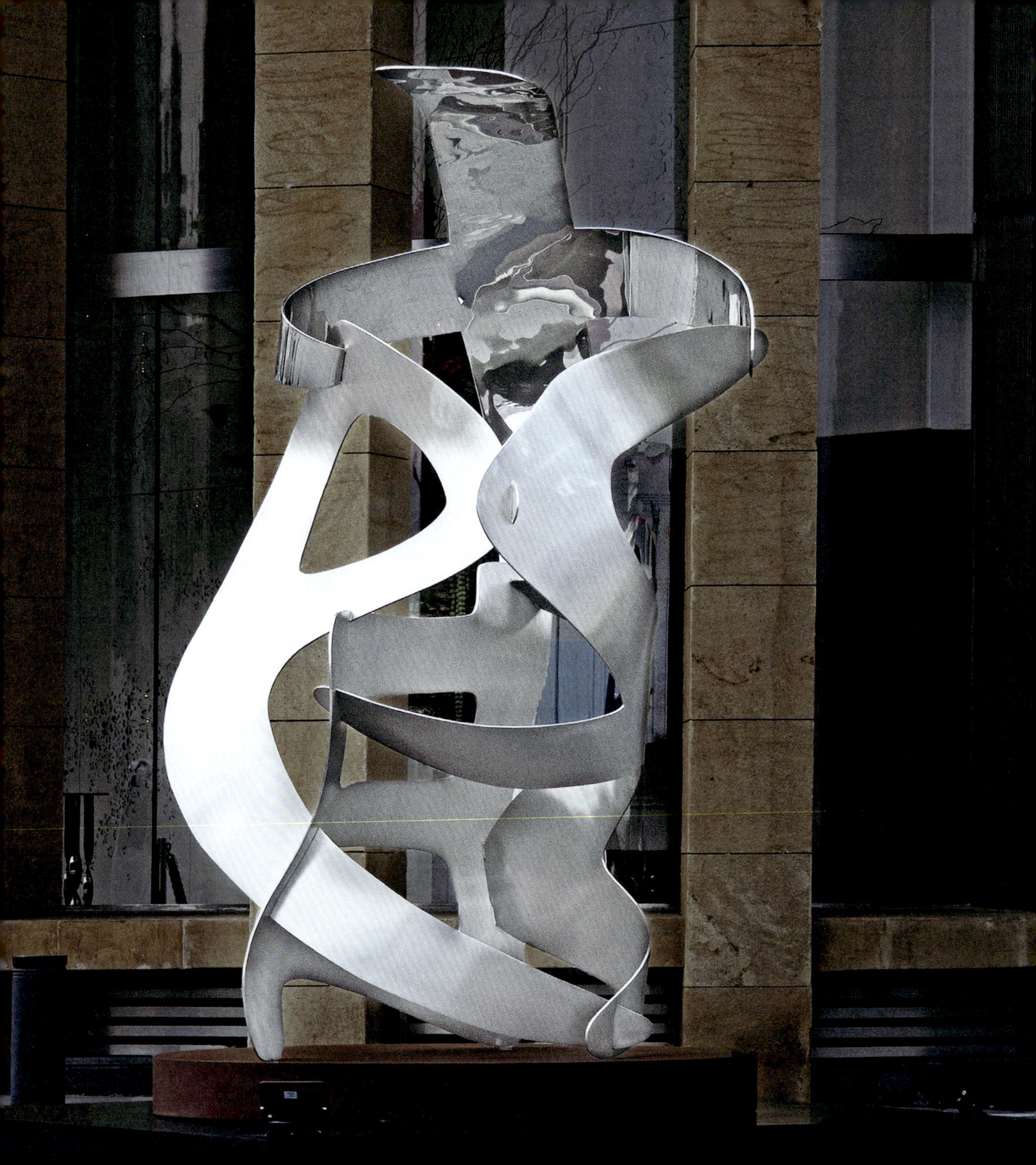

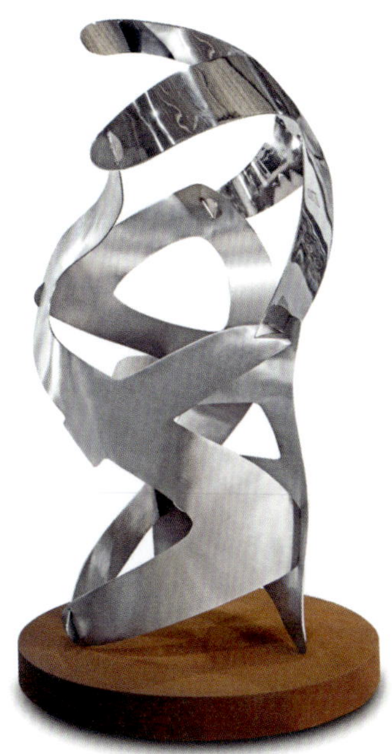

HORRIYA, STAINLESS STEEL, CORTEN AND PAINTED STEEL, 312 X 200 X 200 CM, 2019

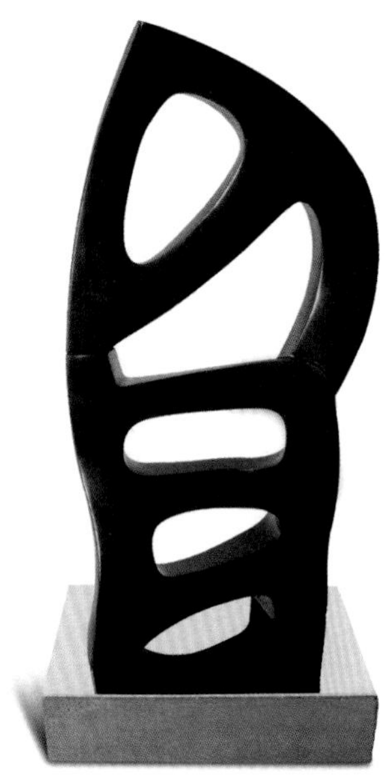

ABOVE: **HOBB**, BRASS, CONCRETE, MIRRORED STAINLESS STEEL, 38 X 19 X 9 CM, 2017
RIGHT: METAL CAST (BRONZE), CONCRETE, 230 X 100 X 60 CM, 2017

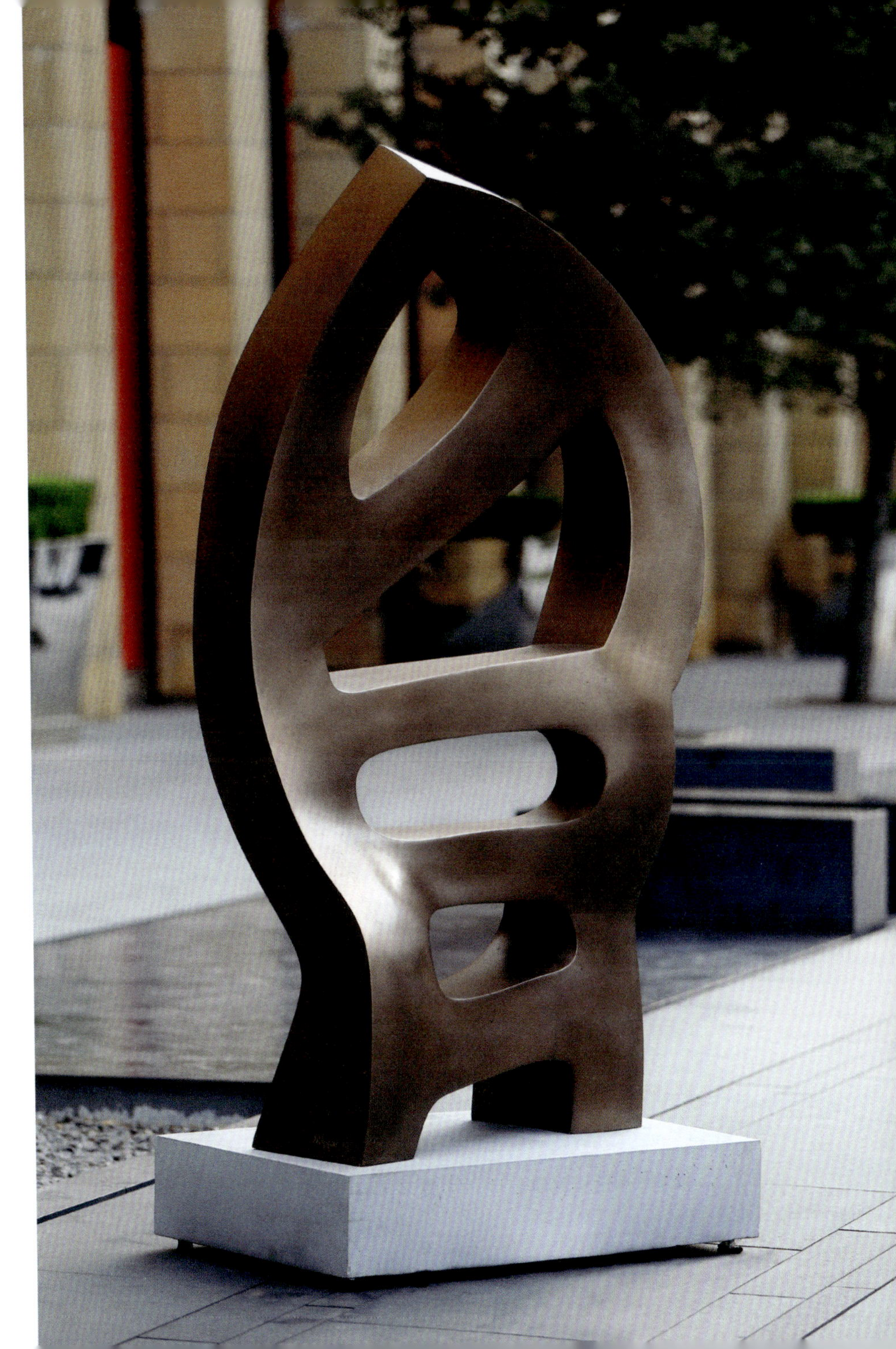

THE ALPHABET

THE ALPHABET

The earliest Phoenician inscription dates from the eleventh century BC, and it is believed the alphabet was in use until the first century BC. During this period, some letters and their meanings varied between different regions and different times. After looking closely at the documented charts, I compiled my own version, using the symbols and meanings I found most relevant. I highlighted the evolution of the letters from Phoenician to Latin (hence all derived languages) as well as Arabic.

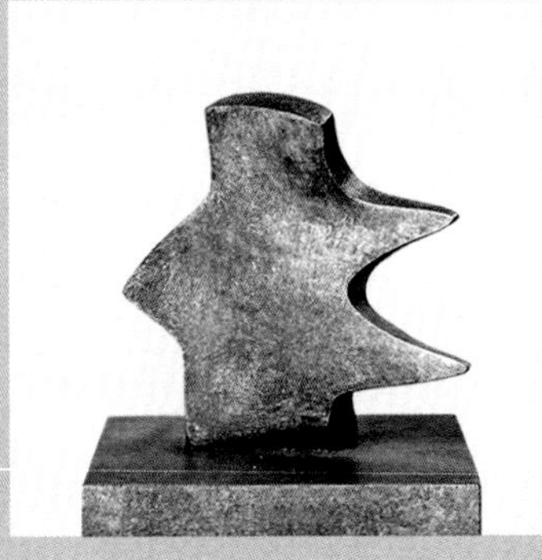

ALEPH is named after and inspired by the Phoenician letter 𐤀, meaning ox, strength, leadership.
𐤀 is the origin of letters '**A**' in Latin and '**ا**' in Arabic.

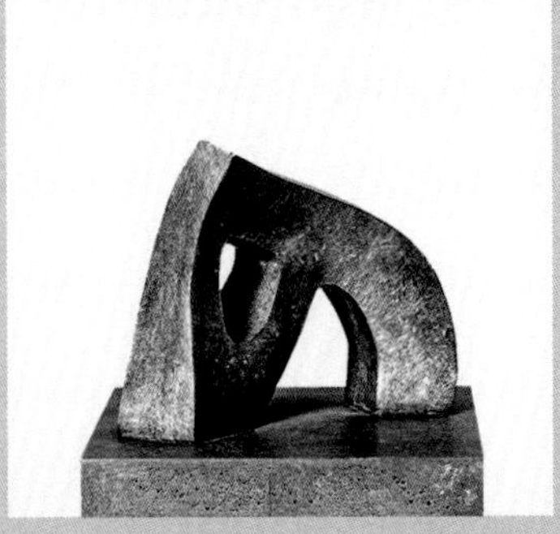

BETH is named after and inspired by the Phoenician letter 𐤁, meaning house, interiority.
𐤁 is the origin of letters '**B**' in Latin and '**ب**' in Arabic.

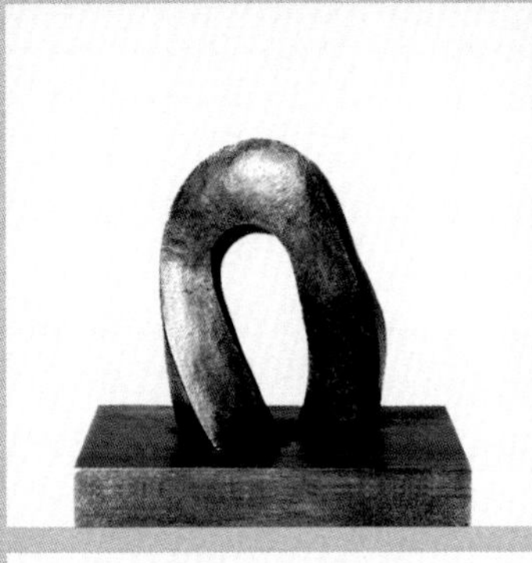

GIMEL is named after and inspired by the Phoenician letter ⅄,
meaning camel, pride.
⅄ is the origin of letters '**C**, **G**' in Latin and '**ح**' in Arabic.

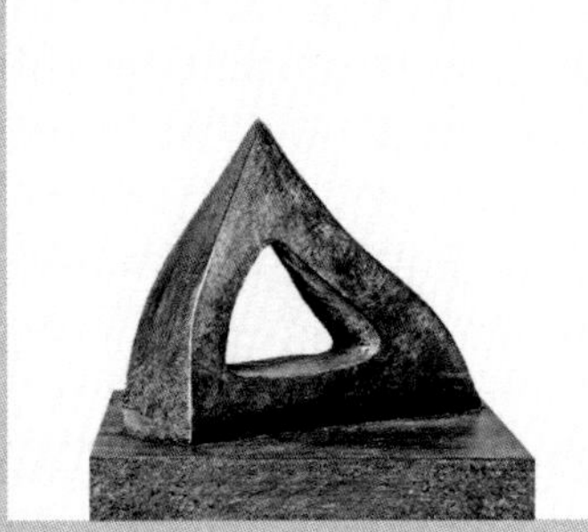

DALETH is named after and inspired by the Phoenician letter ◁,
meaning door, pathway, exteriority.
◁ is the origin of letters '**D**' in Latin and '**ذ، د**' in Arabic.

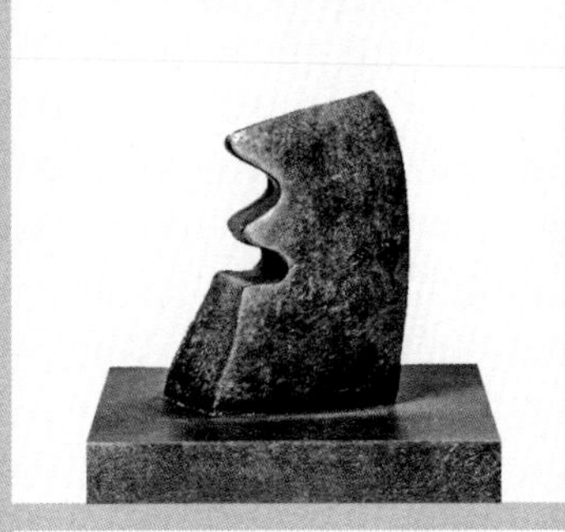

HÉ is named after and inspired by the Phoenician letter ∃,
meaning window, breath, life.
∃ is the origin of letters '**E**, **H**' in Latin and '**ه**' in Arabic.

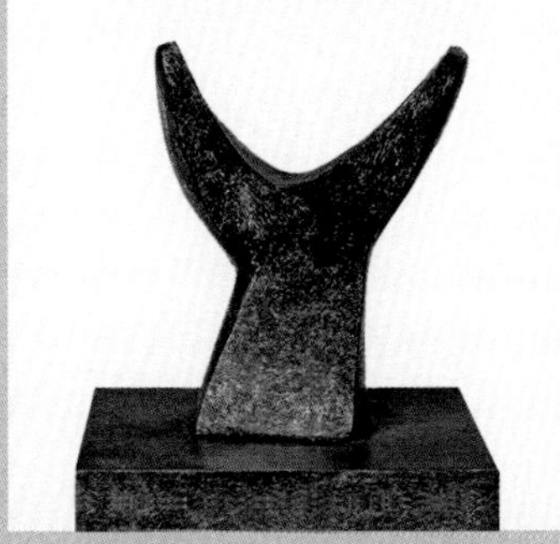

WAW is named after and inspired by the Phoenician letter Ƴ,
meaning nail, hook, secure.
Ƴ is the origin of letters '**F**, **U**, **V**, **W**, **Y**' in Latin and '**و**' in Arabic.

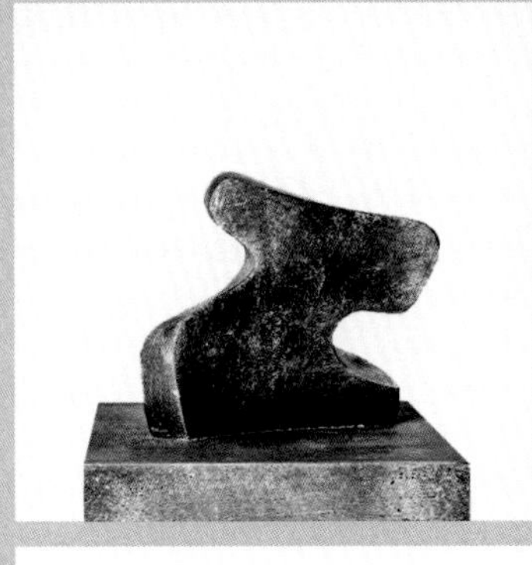

ZAYIN is named after and inspired by the Phoenician letter Ⅰ, meaning weapon, conflict.

Ⅰ is the origin of letters 'Z' in Latin and 'ز' in Arabic.

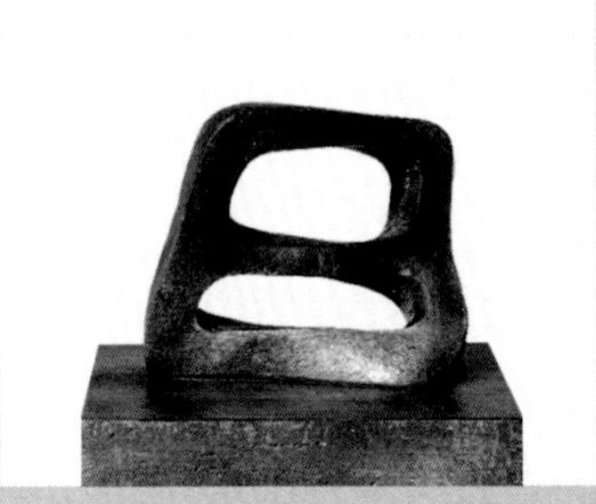

HETH is named after and inspired by the Phoenician letter ⊟, meaning wall, fence, obstacle.

⊟ is the origin of letters 'H' in Latin and 'خ, ح' in Arabic.

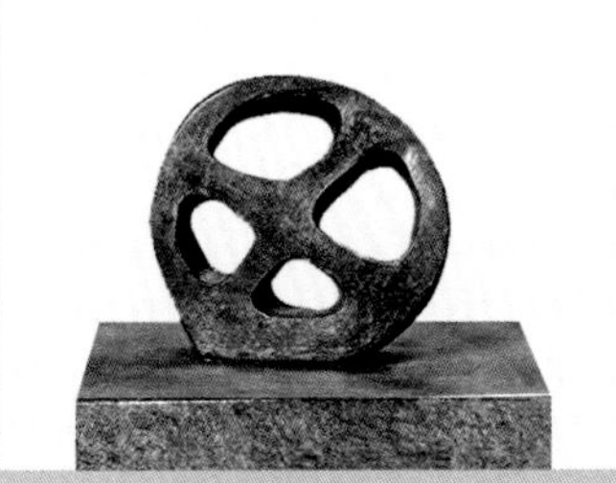

TETH is named after and inspired by the Phoenician letter ⊗, meaning unknown, shield, wheel.

⊗ is the origin of letters 'T' in Latin and 'ط, ظ' in Arabic.

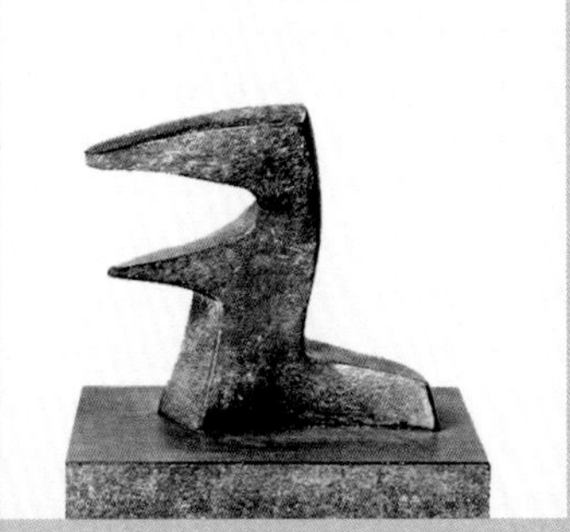

YODH is named after and inspired by the Phoenician letter ⟋, meaning hand, command.

⟋ is the origin of letters 'I, J, Y' in Latin and 'ي' in Arabic.

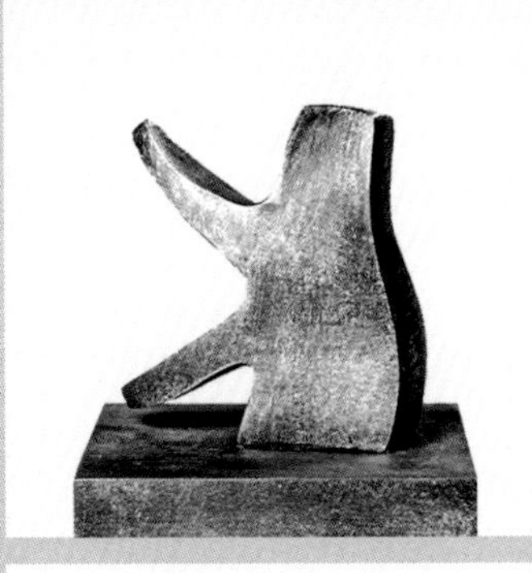

KAPH is named after and inspired by the Phoenician letter ⅄,
meaning palm of hand, bend.
⅄ is the origin of letters '**K**' in Latin and '**ك**' in Arabic.

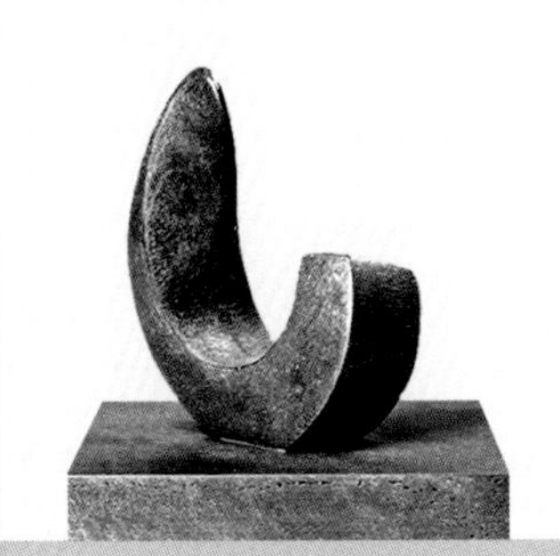

LAMED is named after and inspired by the Phoenician letter ∟,
meaning ox-goad, sting.
∟ is the origin of letters '**L**' in Latin and '**ل**' in Arabic.

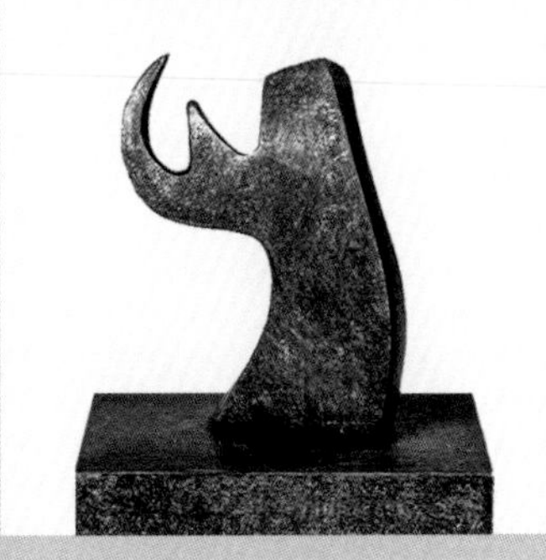

MEM is named after and inspired by the Phoenician letter ⱽ,
meaning water, movement.
ⱽ is the origin of letters '**M**' in Latin and '**م**' in Arabic.

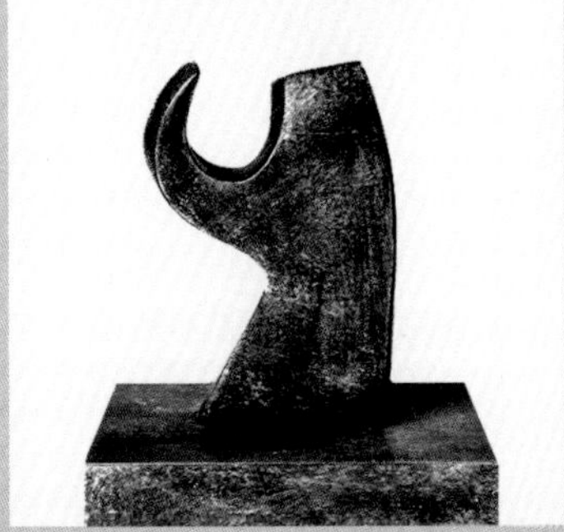

NUN is named after and inspired by the Phoenician letter ⅃,
meaning fish, snake, hidden.
⅃ is the origin of letters '**N**' in Latin and '**ن**' in Arabic.

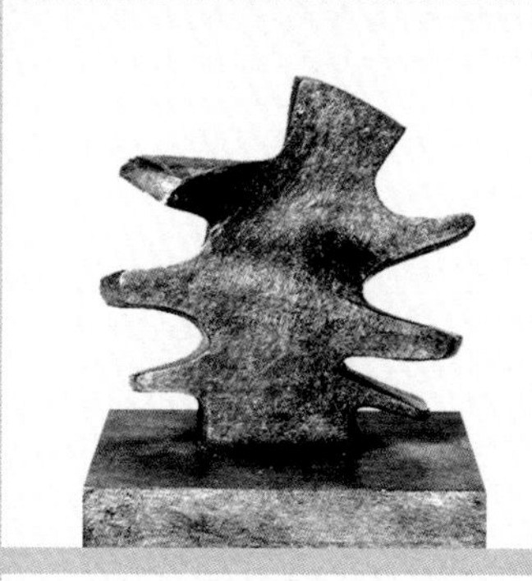

SAMEK is named after and inspired by the Phoenician letter ‡,
meaning support, fishbone.
‡ is the origin of letters '**S, X**' in Latin and '**س**' in Arabic.

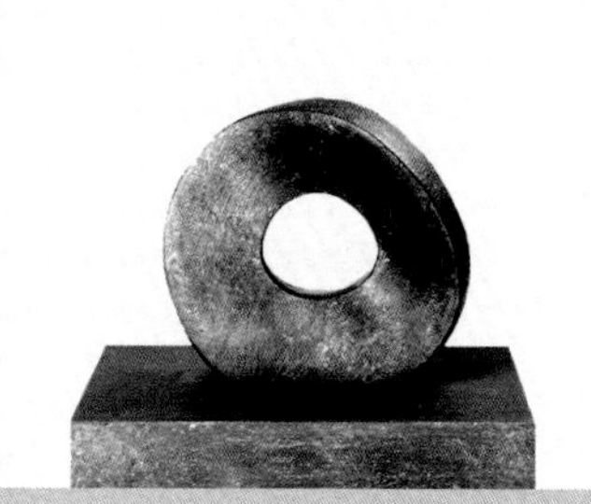

AYIN is named after and inspired by the Phoenician letter O,
meaning eye, see, experience.
O is the origin of letters '**O**' in Latin and '**غ , ع**' in Arabic.

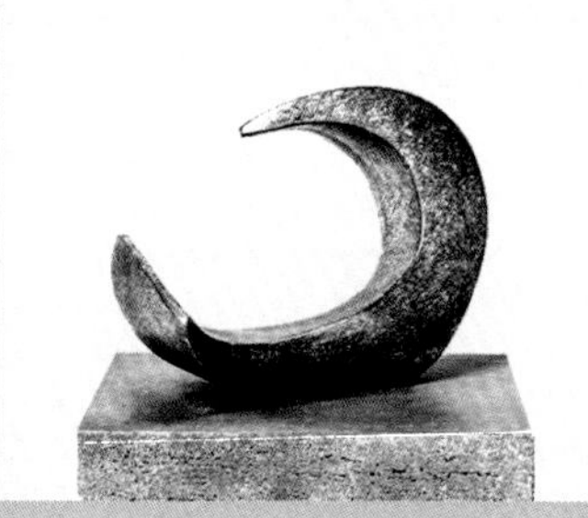

PEH is named after and inspired by the Phoenician letter ⁀,
meaning mouth, word, opening.
⁀ is the origin of letters '**P**' in Latin and '**ف**' in Arabic.

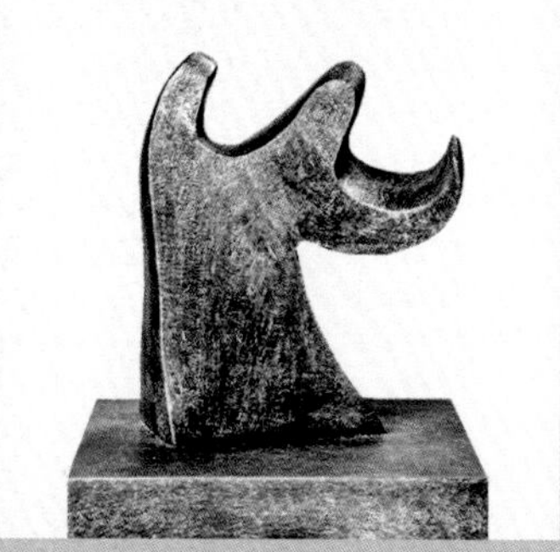

SADHE is named after and inspired by the Phoenician letter ⱽ,
meaning hook, capture.
ⱽ is the origin of letters '**S**' in Latin and '**ص , ض**' in Arabic.

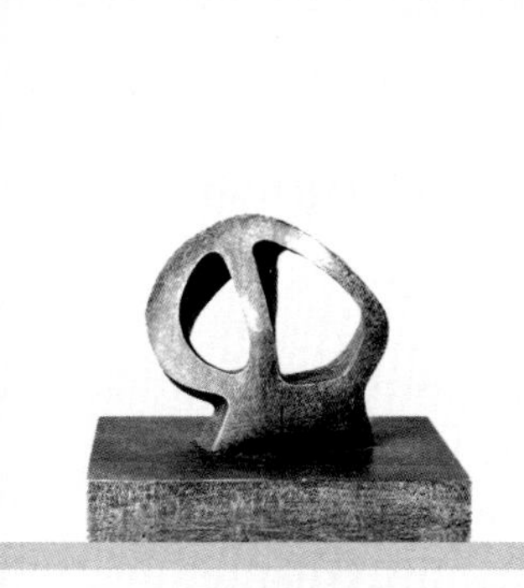

QOPH is named after and inspired by the Phoenician letter ϙ, meaning cut, break, monkey.
ϙ is the origin of letters '**Q**' in Latin and 'ق' in Arabic.

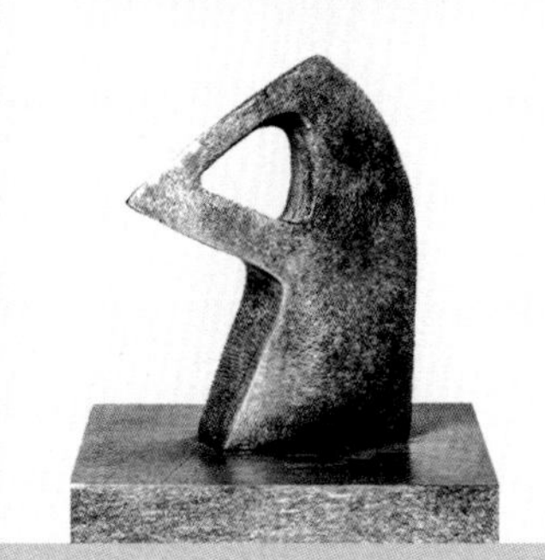

RESH is named after and inspired by the Phoenician letter ᑫ, meaning head, beginning.
ᑫ is the origin of letters '**R**' in Latin and 'ر' in Arabic.

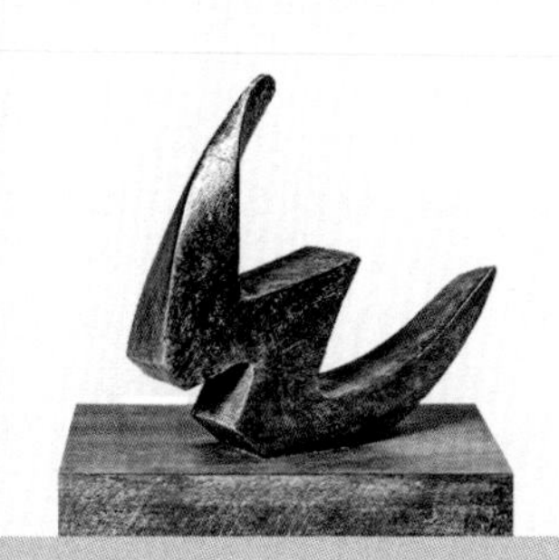

SHIN is named after and inspired by the Phoenician letter ѡ, meaning tooth, consume.
ѡ is the origin of letters '**S, SH**' in Latin and 'ش' in Arabic.

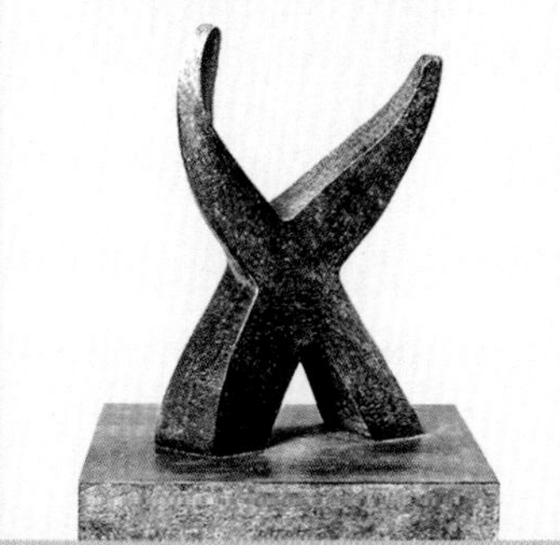

TAW is named after and inspired by the Phoenician letter ✕, meaning mark, sign, connection.
✕ is the origin of letters '**T**' in Latin and 'ث , ت' in Arabic.

'IF I DARE REMIND MY COUNTRYMEN

OF OUR PHOENICIAN FOREFATHERS,

IT IS BECAUSE, BACK IN THEIR HEYDAY,

LONG BEFORE WE EVER BECAME

MERE MUSLIMS AND CHRISTIANS,

WE WERE A SINGLE NATION

AT THE FOREFRONT OF HISTORY,

UNITED IN A SINGLE GLORIOUS PAST.'

'SI JE RAPPELLE AUX MIENS

NOS AÏEUX PHÉNICIENS,

C'EST QU'ALORS NOUS N'ÉTIONS

AU FRONTON DE L'HISTOIRE,

AVANT DE DEVENIR

MUSULMANS OU CHRÉTIENS,

QU'UN MÊME PEUPLE UNI

DANS UNE MÊME GLOIRE.'

FROM 'LA MONTAGNE INSPIRÉE', 1934.
BY CHARLES CORM (1894–1963), FOUNDER OF 'LA REVUE PHÉNICIENNE' IN 1919

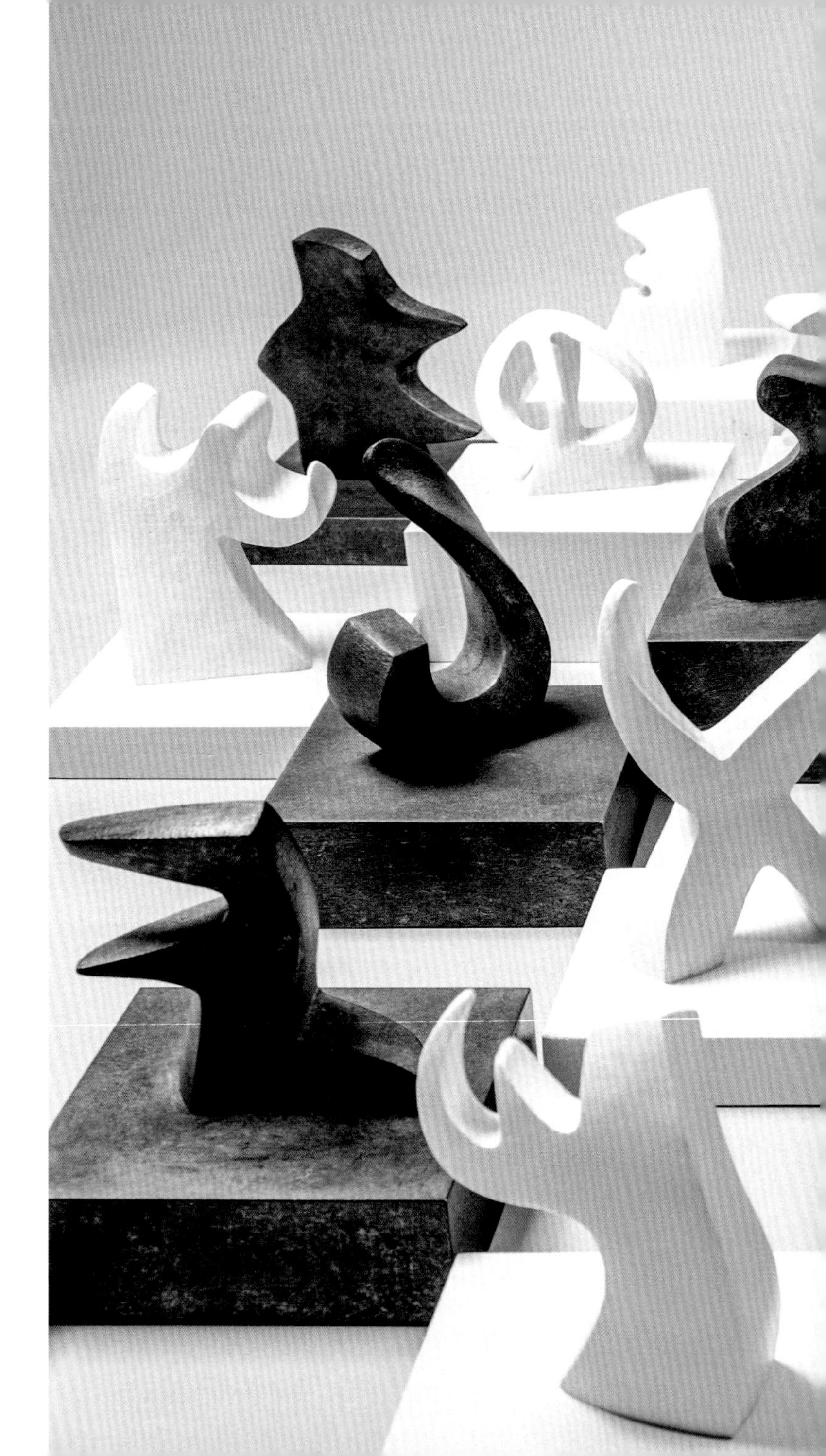

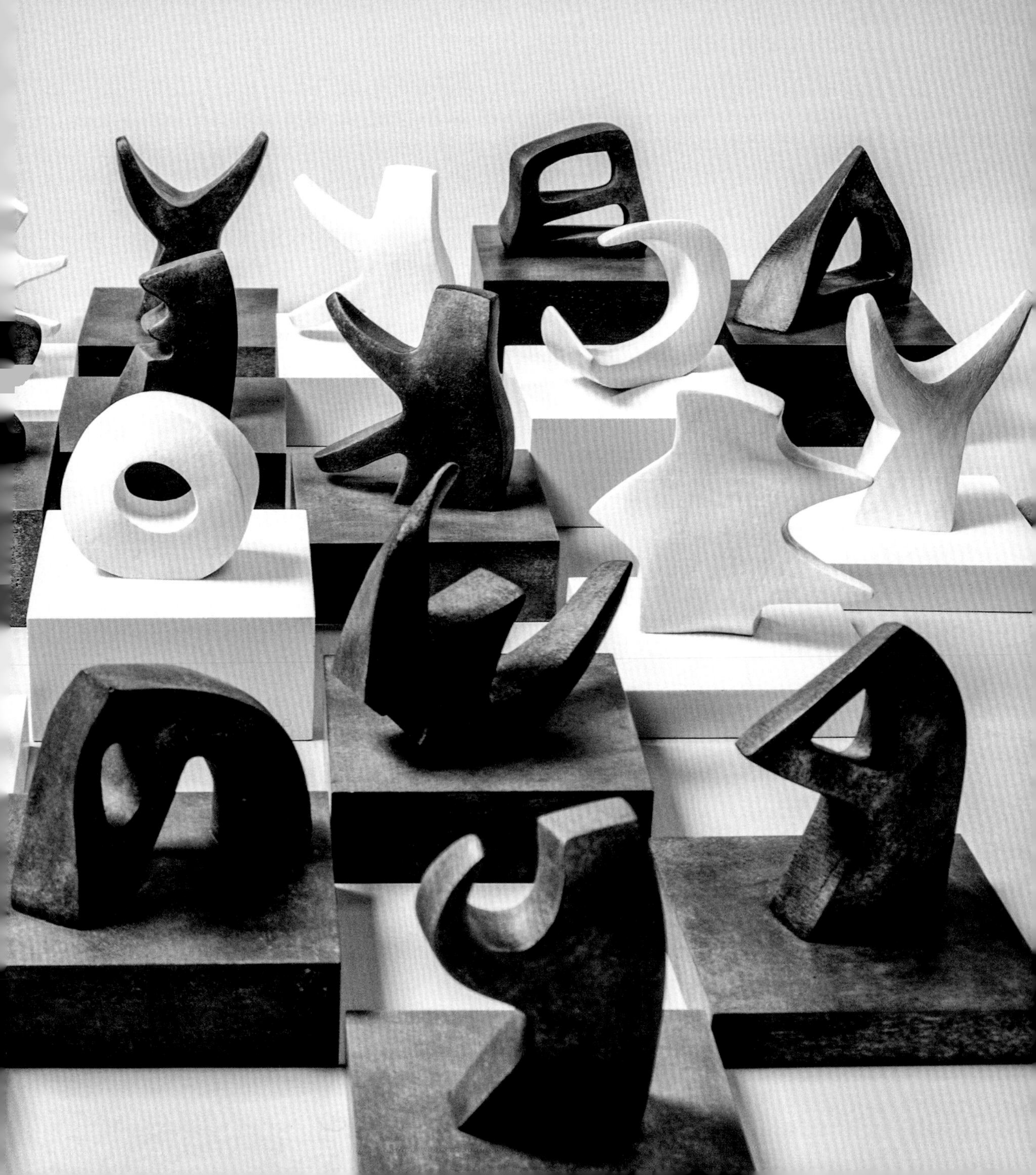

EDITED BY ROSE ISSA
PRODUCTION: Francesca Ricci
PHOTOS: Jean Moraros: cover,
pp. 2-3, 6-7, 11-12, 22, 38, 40-43, 72-73
Naji Zahar: pp. 49, 88-89
George Haddad: pp. 44-45, 48-50, 52,
60-66, 68, 70-71, 80-81, 98-103, 106
Noel Nasr: pp. 17, 39, 45
Wael Khoury: pp. 20, 25, 29-30,
53-55, 58, 77-78, 80, 83, 85-87, 92- 94
Sueraya Shaheen: back cover
DESIGN: normal industries
COPY-EDITOR: Brian David

Printed and Bound in Wales by Gomer

ISBN 978-614-8035-56-2

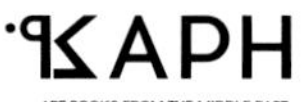

Rue Gouraud, Gemmayze
Immeuble Renno, 3rd floor
Beirut, Lebanon
Tel. +961 3 601 123
www.kaphbooks.com

DISTRIBUTION:
Les Presses du Réel, France
www.lespressesdureel.com

Idea Books, Netherlands
www.ideabooks.nl

ARTBOOK | D.A.P.
75 Broad Street, Suite 630
New York, NY 10004
www.artbook.com

CIEL book distribution, Dubaï, UAE
www.ciel.me